Greetings from TAMPA

Schiffer Publishing Ltd®
4880 Lower Valley Road, Atglen, Pennsylvania 19310

Donald D. Spencer

Other Schiffer Books by Donald Spencer:
Greetings from St. Augustine, 978-0-7643-2802-2, $24.95
Greetings from Daytona Beach, 978-0-7643-2806-0, $24.95
Greetings from Ormond Beach, 978-0-7643-2809-1, $24.95

Other Schiffer Books on Related Subjects
Greetings from St. Petersburg, 978-0-7643-2690-5, $24.95
Miami Beach Postcards, 0-7643-2306-7, $14.95
And for other great titles, please visit our website at www.schifferbooks.com.

Library of Congress Control Number: 2007937585

Designed by Martha Tyzenhouse
Type set in Benguiat Bk BT / New Baskerville
ISBN: 978-0-7643-2898-5
Printed in China

Published by Schiffer Publishing Ltd.
4880 Lower Valley Road
Atglen, PA 19310
Phone: (610) 593-1777; Fax: (610) 593-2002
E-mail: Info@schifferbooks.com

For the largest selection of fine reference books on this and related subjects, please visit our web site at **www.schifferbooks.com**
We are always looking for people to write books on new and related subjects. If you have an idea for a book please contact us at the above address.

This book may be purchased from the publisher.
Include $3.95 for shipping.
Please try your bookstore first.
You may write for a free catalog.

In Europe, Schiffer books are distributed by
Bushwood Books
6 Marksbury Ave.
Kew Gardens
Surrey TW9 4JF England
Phone: 44 (0) 20 8392-8585; Fax: 44 (0) 20 8392-9876
E-mail: info@bushwoodbooks.co.uk
Website: www.bushwoodbooks.co.uk
Free postage in the U.K., Europe; air mail at cost.

Contents

Introduction

Tampa, the county seat of Hillsborough County, started as an Indian village discovered by Spanish explorers in the sixteenth century. England held title to this area during the eighteenth century, leaving a legacy in such names as the Hillsborough River. The community began taking permanent shape in 1824, when Fort Brooke was established at the mouth of the river in present-day downtown Tampa. During the Civil War, the Confederates yielded the fort after bombardment by Union gunboats. In 1880, Tampa was but a little known fishing village of around seven hundred people; however, Henry B. Plant's railroad arrived in 1885 and stimulated new industry. Plant developed the port extensively and promoted tourism. Soon the area was populated by a lively mix of Cubans, Germans, Irish, Italians, Scots, Spaniards and native Southerners attracted to opportunities on this new frontier. Vincent M. Ybor and Ignancio Haya introduced cigar manufacturing in 1886, and cigars are still made in Ybor City, Tampa's Latin Quarter. Tampa was the embarkation point in 1898 for Col. Theodore Roosevelt's Cuba-bound troops. In the 1920s the man-made Davis Islands were created in the bay for resort facilities. Citrus and phosphates accounted for much of the port traffic. Every year, Tampa stages a great midwinter festival known as Gasparilla Carnival, which, for merrymaking, rivals the famous Mardi Gras in New Orleans. The Gandy Bridge opened in 1924 connecting Tampa with St. Petersburg. The Davis Causeway across the northern end of Tampa Bay opened in 1934, providing a short route to Clearwater and the Gulf beaches.

Tampa, one of Florida's largest cities, now has a wide range of industry, is a major distribution center, has a substantial International port, and a major International airport.

This book is a pictorial collection of Tampa's past in an informative and entertaining fashion. It is a factual representation of the city's history made up of postcards. Each authentic postcard illustration is captioned with a brief description of the view. It can be used as an addition to Tampa's history or as a nostalgic tour through the city's past. It is a delightful stroll down memory lane. But more importantly, it enables younger generations to learn about the city simply and enjoyably.

I hope readers of this book will come to appreciate and understand a little better the Tampa of the past.

A Time-line of Tampa's History

Before 1900

1528: Europeans began their first major exploration of North America from the west coast of Florida in the Tampa Bay area, when Spanish explorer Panfilo de Narvaez brought over four hundred people, many of them soldiers.
1539: The Hernando De Soto expedition arrived near Tampa Bay.
1549: Four Dominican friars came to Tampa Bay to establish missions. They were killed by Indians.
1566: Pedro Menendez, founder of St. Augustine, established forts and missions on the west coast of Florida, including Tocobago in the Tampa Bay area.
1763: The British acquired Florida in exchange for Havana.
1775: The first British map was published showing Hillsborough River and Bay.
1782: Pirates, including Jose Gaspar (Gasparilla), started raiding ships along the west coast of Florida.
1818: The First Seminole War occurred.
1821: The powerful *U.S.S. Enterprise*, a warship of the United States, sunk Gasparilla's ship.
1824: Fort Brooke was established at the mouth of Hillsborough River as an Army outpost checking on the Seminole Indians and runaway slaves.
• A natural spring near present-day Ybor City was used by Fort Brooke troops. It soon became known as Government Spring.
1831: The first post office called Tampa Bay was established. In 1834 its name was shortened to Tampa.
1835: Major Francis Dade, with one hundred six soldiers, departed from Fort Brooke on what proved to be a fatal expedition.
• The Second Seminole War started; it lasted seven years.

Greetings From Tampa. Circa 1940s, $3-5.

Greetings From Tampa. Circa 1940s, $3-5.

Greetings From Tampa. Circa 1940s, $3-5.

Greetings From Tampa. Circa 1930s, $3-5.

1837: Fort Brooke was made the headquarters for the Army.
• The first hotel in Tampa opened, aptly named The Tampa Hotel.
• Tampa City was mapped out by Developer Augustus Steele. The first lot sold for $60.
1842: The Second Seminole War ended.
1843: Merchant William G. Ferris established the first general merchandise store in Tampa.
1845: Florida became a state.
1846: The first ferry was built across the Hillsborough River.
1847: Captain James McKay built the first sawmill.
1848: A wood-framed courthouse replaced the log courthouse that was burned by Seminole Indians in 1834.
• A devastating hurricane flooded today's downtown Tampa with fifteen feet of water. Most of the structures in Fort Brooke were destroyed.
• Tampa's first school opened in the courthouse with fourteen students.
1850: Oakland Cemetery, the first public burial ground, was established.
The population was four hundred forty-one; of that, one hundred seventy-nine were slaves.
1851: The First Methodist Church was built in Tampa.
1853: Merchant Jesse Carter established the first stagecoach line between Tampa and Gainesville.
• Publisher Henry Crane established Tampa's first newspaper, the Tampa Herald, and it began its publication in 1854.
1855: Tampa was incorporated as a city—its population was three hundred.
• A new wood-frame courthouse was built.
1856: In the midst of the Third Seminole War, Joseph B. Lancaster was elected the first mayor of Tampa.
1859: Schools reopened after a two-year shutdown due to yellow fever.
• Tampa's first census revealed 885 residents.
1860: Tampa recorded the first hanging.
1861: Florida seceded from the Union and joined the Confederacy. Tampa and Fort Brooke later came under siege from federal naval forces.
1862: Tampa's newly elected mayor, John Jackson, had served only nineteen days when the Confederate military took over the town.
1864: A Union officer reported, "Tampa is desolate in the extreme."
1869: Wealthy resident John T. Lesley ran for mayor of Tampa on a platform to abolish city government and won.
• U.S. troops departed Tampa.
1874: Josiah C. Hanna built the first bridge over Hillsborough River near what is now Nebraska Avenue.
1881: Phosphate was discovered in Tampa.
1883: The Bank of Tampa opened.
• Fort Brooke was closed.
1884: The first Opera House opened in Tampa.
• The first ice plant opened.
• Judge N.G. Buff opened the Palmetto Hotel.
• Henry B. Plant brought his railroad into town, and in 1885, extended it to Port Tampa.
1886: The Bank of Tampa became the First National Bank of Tampa.
• The Plant Steamship Company started service to Cuba.
• S. H. Platt of Hyde Park, Illinois opened Hyde Park in Tampa.
• Vicent Martinez Ybor and Ignacio Haya completed construction of Tampa's first cigar factories Ybor City.
• Vicente Martinez Ybor established a steamboat route from Havana to Tampa via Key West, bringing hundreds of Cuban workers on the SS Hutchison.
• The Cherokee Club, a hotel and gambling casino, opened in Ybor City.
• Steam-powered streetcars connected the village of Tampa with Ybor and Haya's industrial neighborhood.
1887: The City of Tampa was chartered for the second time. The "new" city included four wards: downtown, Hyde Park, Tampa Heights and Ybor City.
• Tampa was made a port of entry.
• The newspaper Cuba started publication in Ybor City.
• The first street railway was established, a narrow gauge line between Tampa and Ybor City.
• A yellow fever epidemic hit Tampa.
1889: Tampa had city water and the first passenger bridge was built over Hillsborough River.
1890: The population of Tampa is 5,532.
• Henry B. Plant started the first Tampa fair.
• Franklin Street was paved with Cypress blocks.
• A new city jail opened.
• Manuel Menendez opened the great restaurant Las Novedadas in Ybor City.
1891: A brick courthouse replaced the wood-frame structure.
• Henry B. Plant's fantastic Tampa Bay Hotel opened alongside Hillsborough River, giving railroad passengers a resort destination.
1892: Electric streetcar service linked downtown Tampa, Ybor City, West Tampa and Ballast Point.
• The West Tampa area was first surveyed and platted (planned), and in 1893, was incorporated with 2,815 residents.
1893: The Tampa Times was first published.
1894: There were 3,000 workers in Tampa's cigar industry.
1895: The Tampa Morning Tribune was circulated as an area newspaper.
• The Cuban Revolution began. The written message to start the revolution was sent to Cuban "insurrectos" via West Tampa, where it was rolled into a cigar to be smuggled to Cuba.
1896: The Florida Brewing Company, Florida's first brewery, was incorporated on Fifth Avenue in Ybor City. The brewery used water from the nearby Government Spring.
1898: The Spanish-American War began and ended; it brought 40,000 Cuba-bound troops to Tampa.
1899: Workers in the Ybor-Mantara factory went on strike after scales were introduced in the factory.
• Henry B. Plant died in New York.

1900 to 1919

1900: There were about one hundred fifty cigar factories in Ybor City and West Tampa.
• Tampa got its first paved streets and had a population of 15,838 residents.
• Tampa had 21.5 miles of trolley tracks.
• West Tampa had more inhabitants than Tallahassee.
1901: The first automobile appeared on Tampa streets.
• Cigar makers created their own union, La Resistencia; they later went on strike, which lasted four months.
1902: telephone service began with seven hundred subscribers.
• The Atlantic Coastline Railway acquired the Plant System.
1904: A new Post Office building was constructed, and the American National Bank of Tampa opened.
• The streetcar line was extended from Ballast Point to Port Tampa.
• A fire consumed one hundred thirty buildings in West Tampa, including homes, businesses, and cigar factories.
• Tampa held the first Gasparilla Celebration.
1905: Casimiro Hernandez opened the Columbia Restaurant in Ybor City, and the City of Tampa purchased the Tampa Bay Hotel for $125,000.
• The Elk's Club opened a lodge in a modified residential home.
1908: The first large steamship docked in Tampa.
• Fire destroyed a seventeen-block area in Ybor City. It was the worst fire in Tampa's history.
1909: Horace Williams won the Tampa-to-Jacksonville Auto Race in 5.3 hours, at a blazing 10 mph average speed.
1910: Another strike paralyzed the cigar industry.
West Tampa had a population of 8,258.
• Tampa was connected to Plant City via a nine-foot ribbon of brick.
1911: Tampa's Confederate War Monument was dedicated at Courthouse Square.
1912: With a population of over 10,000 people, West Tampa was Florida's fifth largest city.
• A new Union Depot was built.
1913: A steel Lafayette Bridge replaced the wooden bridge over Hillsborough River.
• The Hillsborough Hotel opened, and the Elk's Club opened an elegant red brick lodge building.
• Jessamine Flowers Link founded the nation's second Girl Scout troop in Tampa.
1914: Tony Jannus, a 24-year old pilot from Washington, D.C., flew his Benoist airplane from St. Petersburg to Tampa. Later hailed as the birth of commercial aviation, Jannus' New Year's Day journey was the first scheduled flight of the St. Petersburg-Tampa Airboat Line.
1916: The first steamship was built in Tampa, and Babe Ruth signed with the Boston Red Sox at the Tampa Bay Hotel.
1917: The Tampa Public Library opened.
• Ransom E. Olds started the village of Oldsmar.
• Tampa's most famous movie, *Birth of a Race*, was filmed at Sulphur Springs.
1918: Tampa residents received the shocking news that the city's own namesake vessel, the *U.S.S. Tampa*, had been sunk in the faraway theater of war.
• Another destructive fire tore through Tampa, destroying one hundred buildings.
• L'Unione Italiana, an Italian Club, was constructed in Ybor City.
1919: The Tin Can Tourists of the World was organized in Tampa at De Soto Park.
• At Plant Field, Babe Ruth hit a 587-foot home run.

1920 to 1949

1920: Tampa's cigar industry suffered a general strike and all the cigar factories closed.
1921: A vicious hurricane flooded some sections of Tampa.
• The Memorial Highway opened.
1922: The port of Tampa was developed.
• Radio came to Tampa, and Bayshore Boulevard opened as a two-lane drive.
1923: The city limits of Tampa were extended to include the community of Sulphur Springs.
• Professional baseball teams started spring training at Tampa's Plant Field.
1924: The Gandy Bridge across Old Tampa Bay connected Tampa and St. Petersburg.
1925: D.P. Davis pulled off a spectacular "boom time" development by dredging Davis Islands from Hillsborough Bay.
• West Tampa was annexed to the city of Tampa, and Temple Terrace was incorporated as a city.
• Josiah Richardson constructed the Nebraska Hotel (Sulphur Springs Hotel and Arcade).
1926: The Tampa Theater and Tampa Terrace Hotel opened.
• The Hillsborough County Jail opened.
1927: Josiah Richardson built the 225-foot high Sulphur Springs water tower.
• Municipal Hospital opened on Davis Island.
• Falor's, a popular hangout for young people, opened.
• The eighteen-floor Floridian Hotel opened as the tallest hotel in the state.
1928: The population of Tampa was 101,161.
• Hillsborough High School was built.
1929: Tampa factories produced 504,743,000 cigars.
1931: The University of Tampa opened as a junior college.
• Lectors, men and sometimes women, who read to cigar workers while they worked, were barred from Tampa's cigar factories.
• Florida legalized gambling at horse and dog tracks in Tampa and other Florida cities.
1933: The University of Tampa became a four-year university in the old Tampa Bay Hotel.
• Florida legalized slot machines.
1934: Drew Field was purchased by the city of Tampa.
• The Davis Causeway over Old Tampa Bay linked Tampa with Clearwater. The name was changed to Courtney Campbell Parkway in the late 1940s.

1935: WPA (Work Projects Administration) workers constructed a 7,000-foot asphalt runway at Drew Field. (Note: WPA was established by President Roosevelt during the Depression years prior to World War II.)
1936: Over 1.7 million tons of Phosphate was shipped from Tampa.
• The Peter O. Knight Airport opened.
1940: MacDill Air Force Base opened.
• There were 23,052 African-Americans in Tampa.
• The population of Tampa was 108,391.
1941: The U.S. entry into World War II saw Tampa with two major air training bases—MacDill and Drew Field.
1942: World War II took workers from an already slumping cigar industry.
1943: Dale Mabry Highway was opened to connect Drew Field and MacDill Air Force Base.
1945: World War II ended.
• Hillsborough County had 207,844 residents.
1946: National Airlines began service from Tampa to Havana, Cuba.
• The Tampa based Jim Walter Corporation began selling shell homes.
1947: Drew Field became Tampa International Airport.

After 1950

1950: The U.S. Senate's Kefauver Crime Investigating Committee came to town, ripped into public officials who permitted gambling and corruption, and left the cleanup to local good citizens.
• The population of Tampa was 124,681.
1952: A new terminal was opened at Tampa International Airport.
1953: Tampa's population increased overnight from 124,000 to 253,000 when suburbs were annexed through legislative action.
1955: Fidel Castro came to Tampa and spoke to a crowd of three hundred supporters, police officers, and FBI agents.
1959: Busch Gardens opened in Tampa.
1960: The University of South Florida opened its doors to 1,965 students on a new campus.
• The completion of the Howard Frankland Bridge provided another cross-Tampa Bay connection to St. Petersburg.
• Hillsborough County had 397,788 residents while the population of Tampa was 274,970.
1962: President John F. Kennedy banned trade and travel between Cuba and the United States, breaking the vital link between Cuban tobacco and Tampa cigar makers, which further debilitated the already stagnant cigar industry.
1963: President Kennedy visited Tampa four days before his assassination in Dallas.
1967: Tampa Stadium opened with 47,000 seats.
1970: The "Dark Continent" at Busch Gardens was the states' leading attraction.
• Hillsborough County had 490,265 residents, while the population of Tampa was 277,714.
1971: Walt Disney World opened near Orlando, and Tampa's Busch Gardens soon lost its number-one ranking to Mickey Mouse and his friends.
1974: Ybor City was named a historic district on the National Register of Historic Places.
1976: Professional football's Tampa Bay Buccaneers played their first game—a 20-0 loss to Houston.
1977: An inch of snow fell on Tampa on January 19.
1980: Thirty-two people plunged into the bay when a freighter rammed the Sunshine Skyway Bridge and twenty-three Coast Guardsmen died when the U.S. Coast buoy tender Blackthorne collided with the tanker Capricorn in the mouth of the bay.
• Tampa's six operating port facilities ranked third in foreign export tonnage.
• Hillsborough County had 646,960 residents.
• Tampa was the fifty-third largest city in the United States.
1983: West Tampa was named a historic district on the National Register of Historic places.
1984: Tampa hosted its first Super Bowl.
1990: Ybor City was recognized as one of three National Historic Landmark Districts in the State of Florida.
• The massive waterfront Tampa Convention Center opened in the downtown area where Fort Brooke was founded 166 years before.
• Tampa was the site of Super Bowl XXV.

Chapter One:

The City

Battle. Prior to the sixteenth century the Tampa Bay area was settled by several Indian tribes. Friction developed between the native Indians and Spanish conquistadores when the Spanish attempted to invade the area. This postcard illustrates a similar scene from a Cyclorama exhibit in Sarasota County. Circa 1950s, $4-6.

Fort Brooke. Tampa's roots reach back to an Indian fishing village and beyond. Spanish explorer Hernando De Soto sailed into the Tampa Bay area in 1539 searching for gold; he was, at the time, still governor of Cuba. Native tribes called the village by the bay Tanpa, which meant "sticks of fire." On maps done by early explorers, the spelling became Tampa. Fort Brooke, built around the time of the Seminole Indian Wars, attracted traders and settlers, and by 1855, there was a town called Tampa. Circa 1908, $6 8.

Aerial View of Tampa. This view of downtown Tampa shows Hillsborough River, the skyscraper area, Davis Islands, Hillsborough Bay, and the old Florida State Fair Grounds (the race track is shown in the top left corner). Circa 1920s, $2-4.

The Heart of Tampa.
Pictured is the Confederate Monument and a section of Franklin Street. The Confederate Monument, located on the southeast corner of the Hillsborough County Courthouse Square, was dedicated in 1911. It was later moved to the present courthouse. Cancelled 1912, $3-5.

City Skyline.
This view, taken on Davis Islands, shows the skyline of the city in the background. Tampa's skyline reflects its business, industrial development, and prominence as a port on Florida's West Coast. Circa 1940s, $3-5.

Tony Jannus Park. Air transportation was proved financially possible because of the January 1, 1914 flight from St. Petersburg to Tampa. As a reminder of this daring feat, Tampa dedicated a small park in downtown Tampa to the airline's pilot, Anthony "Tony" Jannus. The skyline of Tampa is shown in the background of this postcard view. Circa 1940s, $1-3.

Skyline View of Tampa. The moonlit Hillsborough River was a memorable scene for visitors looking in the direction of downtown Tampa, as it provided charm to this beautiful skyline. Circa 1940s, $3-5.

Davis Islands. In 1924, D. P. Davis developed residential property from the sand flats at the mouth of Hillsborough River. Sand pumped from Hillsborough Bay developed the islands (center of this postcard view). The original Municipal airport terminal on Davis Islands, known as Peter O. Knight Airport, was the major airport for the city of Tampa. Built in 1936, the airport was demolished in 1964. Circa 1938, $1-3.

Tampa Skyline from Davis Islands. A view of the Tampa skyline taken from Davis Islands. Circa 1940s, $2-4.

Panoramic View of Downtown Tampa. Circa 1940s, $2-4.

Chapter Two:

Changing Streets and Byways

Hyde Park. In 1886 S. H. Platt purchased twenty acres of land and named it Hyde Park. Convenient to downtown Tampa, it became the oldest platted residential area west of Hillsborough River. Shown here is a view along Hyde Park Avenue, a main thoroughfare in the area. Hyde Park was a lovely residential area with no traffic problems. Circa 1910, $1-3.

Early Roads and Streets. Before 1900 many of Tampa's roads and streets were unpaved. Cancelled 1919, $1-3.

Franklin Street Looking South. Tampa's main drag, Franklin Street, looked like this at the turn of the twentieth century. In this scene the Maas Brothers department store is shown on the left; it was founded in 1890 by brothers Abe and Isaac Maas. That same year Franklin Street was paved with Cypress blocks. Circa 1910, $4-6.

Midwinter Scene. This scene of Lafayette Street Bridge shows the Tampa Bay Hotel and dome of the First Baptist Church in the background. The annual event of Tampa is the landing of Jose Gaspar (Gasparilla) and his pirate crew. The midwinter crowds are enjoying the delightful sunshine while awaiting the arrival of this noted visitor. Circa 1920s, $8-10.

Nighttime Scene on Franklin Street.
Franklin Street was the hub of commerce. This nighttime scene is a view of the street looking south. Circa 1920s, $3-5.

Florida Avenue looking south.
Shown are the Federal Building, Catholic church, Elk's Home and, on the right, the Hillsboro Hotel. Automobile traffic was now starting to pick up in downtown Tampa. Circa 1920s, $3-5.

Franklin Street Looking North. Busy downtown Tampa, looking north on Franklin Street from Courthouse Square. The Hillsborough County Courthouse Square is shown in the bottom right of this postcard view. James A. Wood, who designed the Tampa Bay Hotel, built the courthouse in 1892; it was torn down in 1952. Cancelled 1924, $3-5.

Crowds Crossing Lafayette Street Bridge. The city's skyline, looking east across the Lafayette Street (now Kennedy Boulevard) Bridge—the bridge over Hillsborough River. The town was humming with activity at the time because of the excitement of the Florida real estate boom. Circa 1920s, $3-5.

Franklin Street Looking North. The main street in the shopping and commercial center of the city bristles with neon and painted sidewalk signs, marble and glass store fronts, tall office buildings, and bank structures. Cancelled 1943, $3-5.

Looking North on Florida Avenue. There was diagonal parking on Florida Avenue, as shown in this postcard view looking north from the City Hall Tower. A corner of the old Hillsborough County Courthouse Square is on the left. Circa 1920s, $3-5.

Bay Shore Drive. Bay Shore Drive opened as a two lane drive. It was later widened and renamed Bayshore Boulevard. Circa 1922, $1-3.

Lafayette Street Bridge. The Lafayette Street (now Kennedy Boulevard) Bridge in the 1930s. This view shows U. S. bombers from MacDill Field Army Air Base flying over the bridge. The minarets of the Tampa Bay Hotel can be seen in the background. Circa 1930s, $3-5.

Aerial View. This postcard shows how Bayshore Boulevard follows a path along the western shoreline of Hillsborough Bay. Circa 1930s, $1-3.

Bayshore Boulevard and Bridge. This view shows the beautiful Bayshore Boulevard and the bridge to Davis Islands. Circa 1930s, $1-3.

Statue. Christopher Columbus Statue on Bayshore Boulevard near downtown Tampa. Cancelled 1957, $1-3.

Bayshore Boulevard. An aerial view of Bayshore Boulevard after it was widened to four lanes with a median and street lights. Circa 1960s, $1-3.

Chapter Three:

Businesses and City Structures

County Courthouse. This view shows the Hillsborough County Courthouse at Franklin and Lafayette streets (now Kennedy Boulevard). The courthouse, built in 1892, cost $60,000. Cancelled 1912, $4-6.

Courthouse and Confederate Monument. The Confederate Monument, a Civil War memorial entitled "Memoria In Aeterna," was a gift in 1911 from United Daughters of the Confederacy. In 1952 this monument was moved to the new Hillsborough County Courthouse. Circa 1915, $3-5.

Federal Building. This structure, built in 1904, was located at Florida Avenue between Twiggs and Zack streets. When Tampa's Post Office and Federal Building was completed, it was the finest government building in all South Florida. Circa 1910, $8-12.

Another View of the Federal Building. Circa 1910, $8-12.

Federal Building and Post Office. The Post Office shared space in the Federal Building. Circa 1930s, $3-5

Evolution of Power. Shown in this view is the Tampa Electric Company power plant, built in 1904. Some years later, the plant was enlarged and had two stacks. Before the plant was torn down in 1970, it had run with three smoke-stacks for years. The Tampa Tribune building now occupies this location. Circa 1904, $4-6.

Citizens Bank Building. The Citizens Bank and Trust Company building opened for business in 1913. This ten-story brick building was one of Tampa's first skyscrapers. Circa 1915, $2-4.

YMCA Building. The sturdy YMCA building on Florida Avenue. This structure has served generations of Tampa residents since it was built in 1908. The great orator and politician William Jennings Bryan spoke at the dedication. Circa 1910, $3-5.

Free Library. The Tampa Free Library, located at Franklin Street and Seventh Avenue, was completed in 1915. Designed by architect Fred James, it was a one-story building with a basement and buff brick. A marble archway with white Doric columns framed the entrance. The library was founded with a Carnegie fund and originally contained 64,000 volumes. Cancelled 1920, $6-8.

Tampa City Hall. The City Hall, a ten-story structure built in 1915, houses all the offices of city government. Tampa has a representative form of government consisting of a mayor and representatives from various districts of the city. The City Hall is listed on the National Register of Historic Places. Circa 1915, $4-6.

Tampa's Magnificient City Hall.
The City Hall, once Tampa's most impressive structure, is now surrounded by glass-sheathed skyscrapers. The clock tower, known as Hortense, was a donation from the W. H. Beckwith Jewelry Company. Circa 1920s, $3-5.

City Hall and Confederate Monument. The Tampa City Hall (in the background) and the Confederate Monument on old Courthouse Square at Franklin and Lafayette streets (now Kennedy Boulevard). The monument was moved to the new site of the Hillsborough County Courthouse when it was built in 1952. Circa 1930s, $4-6.

Grand View of Four Important Buildings. The distinctive style of the first brick Hillsborough County Courthouse, shown in this view, echoed the minarets of the grand Tampa Bay Hotel. Both buildings were designed by architect James A. Wood, who came from New York at the behest of railroad shipping tycoon Henry B. Plant and stayed to give Tampa some of its more graceful and original structures.

The courthouse was torn down in 1952. Today the site is occupied by the Marine Bank and Trust Company building. Also shown in this view are the Elks Club at the far left, the Tampa Terrace Hotel (tall building in the rear), and Tampa's City Hall, with its clock tower, at the right. Circa 1926, $4-6.

Municipal Hospital. The Municipal Hospital opened on Davis Islands in 1927 and later became Tampa General Hospital. Circa 1930s, $1-3.

Maas Brothers. Maas Brothers opened in downtown Tampa as a "Dry Goods Place" in 1886. By 1905, it had become the city's first complete department store. In the 1950s, Maas Brothers started to branch out, establishing its first shopping mall site in Westshore Plaza in 1966; by 1983, it had nineteen stores in its retail chain. The old Maas Brothers Department Store, at the corner of Franklin and Zack streets, closed in the late 1980s. Cancelled 1931, $4-6.

Rattlesnake. This Hillsborough County community, located at the eastern end approach to Gandy Bridge between Tampa and St. Petersburg, had a post office, store and snake pit. Rattlesnake was named by George K. End, who was the original canner of diamondback rattlesnake. End's tourist stop attracted many motorists for the canned delicacy and to patronize the uniquely-named post office. The community was annexed to Tampa in the 1950s and the name of Rattlesnake disappeared. Circa 1930s, $4-6.

Davis Islands Coliseum.
The landmard, Davis Islands Coliseum, was the scene of many gala events. The facility hosted entertainment of all kinds, including dancing and roller-skating. The structure burned down in the mid 1970s. Circa 1930s, $4-6.

Sanatorio Del Centro Espanol. The Sanatorio del Centro Espanol on Bayshore Boulevard as it appeared in 1904. This club functioned as a mutual aid society where members could receive medical care. Circa 1910s, $4-6.

Municipal Auditorium. With a seating capacity of more than 2,000 the Municipal Auditorium was often used for conventions, plays, concerts, and operas. The sender of this postcard wrote, "I'm in Tampa at the State Music festival with the Glee Club. We are going to sing at this auditorium tomorrow night with Noble Cain as our guest director." Cancelled 1942, $1-3.

Hillsborough County Courthouse. Shown is an overview of the newest Hillsborough County Courthouse. Built in 1952, it replaced the unique, historic 1892 courthouse a few blocks away. It was the fourth home for the county government. The Confederate Monument can be seen on the front lawn. This Civil War memorial was moved here when the building was completed. Cancelled 1955, $1-3.

Chapter Four:

Transportation

Mass Transportation. In 1886, Tampa Street Railway Company provided Tampa with its first form of public transportation. By 1913 Tampa had a unified street car system throughout the city. Shown is a view looking west on Twiggs Street with a glimpse of the Catholic Church of the Sacred Heart and the eight-story, red brick Hillsboro Hotel. Circa 1910, $4-6.

Franklin Street Streetcars. Famous Alligator Border Postcards, published by S. Langsdorf & Co., featuring streetcars on Franklin Street. Circa 1910s, $40-45.

Franklin Street Looking South. A bird's eye view of streetcars on Franklin Street. Traveling by streetcar was not only comfortable and convenient, but it took people from the suburbs to the center of downtown Tampa. Circa 1920s, $2-4.

Lafayette Street Bridge. In 1888, Henry B. Plant convinced the city of Tampa to build a bridge over Hillsborough River at Lafayette Street. Plant purchased land on the river next to the bridge and began building the Tampa Bay Hotel. The bridge shown in this view replaced the original wooden bridge in 1913. A drawbridge lifts to permit passage of river crafts. Also shown is the steamer *Favorite*, a popular steamboat that made regular trips between the communities on Tampa Bay. It was also the favorite means of transportation to the Gulf beaches in the 1920s. Circa 1920s, $3-5.

H. B. Plant Steamboat. The original *H. B. Plant* steamboat carried mail, freight, and passengers to St. Johns River settlements. The steamboat was destroyed by fire in 1890. In 1899 a second *H. B. Plant* was built in Jacksonville. A day boat, it may have served on local runs on St. Johns River, but in June 1901, she was sent to Tampa to run on the Manatee River. The postcard shows the *H. B. Plant* at a St. Petersburg dock. The second *H. B. Plant* burned at a Tampa pier in 1913. Cancelled 1909, $7-9.

Lafayette Street Bridge. Of the seven modern bridges that cross the winding Hillsborough River within greater Tampa, more traffic passes over this span than over any of the other six. Tampa's first, hand-operated, wooden bridge was constructed across Hillsborough River at this same point. Circa 1920s, $2-4.

Steamboats on Tampa Bay.
The first steamboat built on Florida's West Coast was built locally at Big Bayou for trading between Big Bayou, St. Petersburg and Tampa. Fifty-nine feet long, the vessel was launched in 1885. In 1905, F. A. Davis formed the Tampa Bay Transportation Co., featuring the five hundred-passenger steamer *Favorite*. The Independent line, headed by H. Walter Fuller, which operated the steamers *Manatee* and *H. B. Plant*, later acquired the *Favorite*. The steamers *Favorite* and *Manatee* are shown on Tampa Bay in this postcard view. These steamboats were a familiar sight on the Tampa Bay waterfront from 1908 to 1924. Circa 1915, $10-12.

Steamboat Transportation. In the late 1800s and early 1900s steamboats were the main means of transportation for getting from here to there in the Tampa Bay area. They were also a favorite means of transportation for going to the beaches on the Gulf of Mexico. Shown is the steamer *H. B. Plant* leaving St. Petersburg on the way to Tampa. Circa 1920s, $6-8.

A Tourist's View of Port Tampa. In 1893, "The docks at Port Tampa extended a mile or more out in the bay; the cars run out and large vessels load and unload. It makes a lively scene. I saw the steamer from Havana, Cuba come in, and the rush of the passengers and trunks through the custom house." Port Tampa was one of the busiest spots in the nation during the 1890s. Circa 1908, $5-7.

Phosphate Docks at Tampa. A view of Port Tampa. Pictured on the far right is Henry B. Plant's Port Tampa Inn, a novel hotel that extended over the water. Advertisements stated that guests could fish from their windows. A phosphate elevator is shown at the near right. Phosphate is one of Tampa's leading exports. Cancelled 1908, $5-7.

Aerial View of Tampa Docks. This view shows the old Mallory Docks in 1911 at the Hendry & Knight Channel in Tampa's harbor that had just been deepened. Traffic increased, causing the port to become very congested. The Mallory Steamship Line operated steamships to New York, Mobile and Key West. Cancelled 1923, $5-7.

Unloading Bananas. Bananas are brought to Tampa from the plantations of Central America and unloaded at the banana docks. Bananas were not the principal import of Tampa, but they were the most photogenic. Circa 1930s, $2-4.

Preparing Bananas for Transshipment. At Port Tampa, banana boats unload fruit from Central America almost daily. Shown in this view are stevedores transferring bananas from ship to train. Circa 1930, $3-5.

Ocean Freighters Docked at Port Tampa. Steamships from all over the world docked at Port Tampa, which was one of the largest ports between Norfolk and New Orleans. Today, Mammoth freighters transport and deliver a variety of cargoes here, including phosphate, citrus, cattle, sugar, tropical fruits, and fertilizer materials. Circa 1920s, $5-7.

World's First Scheduled Airline. In 1914, Tampa became the site of the world's first regularly scheduled airline. On January 1, Anthony "Tony" Jannus flew a 75-horsepower Benoist seaplane from St. Petersburg to a landing at Hillsborough River in Tampa. The St. Petersburg-Tampa Airboat Line made two to five trips daily charging only five dollars one way per passenger. Photo reproduction. Circa 1960s, $2-4.

First Airline Passenger. Abe Pheil, ex-mayor of St. Petersburg, paid $400 for the honor of being the first passenger on the January 1, 1914 21-mile flight from St. Petersburg to Tampa. Shown are flight organizer Percival Fansler, Pheil, and pilot Anthony "Tony" Jannus posing near the Benoist plane. Photo reproduction. Circa 1960s, $2-4.

Aerial Transportation. The 1914 Benoist airboat flights proved that transporting passengers by air was feasible and safe. It was a preview of things to come in the field of aerial transportation. Circa 1940s, $1-3.

Gandy Bridge. In 1924 the Gandy Bridge opened as the longest automobile toll bridge in the world. It shortened the mileage from Tampa to St. Petersburg from forty-three to nineteen miles. Such a bridge had been dreamed about, but it was George S. Gandy who made that dream a reality. Cancelled 1935, $2-4.

Green Light to the Gulf Beaches. Citizens from both Tampa and St. Petersburg purchased shares of the bridge, which paid for the construction of The Gandy Bridge. The original toll was seventy-five cents per car and driver, with ten cents extra for each passenger. Circa 1940s, $1-3.

Davis Causeway. Built by Ben T. Davis, the Davis Causeway across the northern end of Tampa Bay connected Tampa with Clearwater and the Gulf beaches. Tolls on this causeway were fifty cents round trip for passenger cars. This causeway, which has been in use since 1934, has since been named Courtney Campbell Parkway. The beaches along this causeway are popular for bathing and fishing. Circa 1940s, $2-4.

Picnicking and Fishing. The entire family enjoys an outing on the Courtney Campbell Parkway between Tampa and Clearwater. There are picnic tables and stoves for preparing food, while the children swim and the older adults try their luck at fishing. Circa 1940s, $2-4.

Tampa Union Station. As the end of the twentieth century drew near, trains were still stopping at the modest brick structure serving as Tampa Union Station. The outward appearance of the head house changed little from this postcard view. The depot was built in 1912 to serve the Atlantic Coast Line and the Seaboard Airline railroads. Circa 1914, $6-8.

Tampa International Airport. In the 1960s, air travel to the Tampa-St. Petersburg area began to burgeon and Tampa's airport was selected as the regional airport over the St. Petersburg-Clearwater Airport just across Tampa Bay. Located on the old Drew Field, Tampa International Airport was soon too small for the increased traffic, so a new airport was planned that would be on the cutting edge of airport design. The modern $80 million Tampa International Airport opened in 1971—an airport appropriate for the area that gave birth to commercial aviation. Circa 1970s, $1-3.

Chapter Five:

Waterways

Many Names River. Seminole Indians, who inhabited this part of Florida, called Hillsborough River Lockcha-popka-chiska, meaning "river where one crosses to eat acorns." Pre-Seminole Indians called it the Mocoso River and the Spanish dubbed it the River of San Julian deArriga. In 1769, the British gave it the name by which it is known today—after the Earl of Hillsborough, Britain's colonial secretary at the time. Circa 1908, $2-4.

Picturesque River.
A picturesque view of Hillsborough River near Tampa. Its banks are wooded and artistically hung with Spanish moss. The river is navigable for about ten miles, and is crossed by two draw bridges. Cancelled 1908, $3-5.

Hillsborough River. This scene shows the suspension bridge over the river in the Hillsborough River State Park, near Tampa. The verdant tropical setting of this park makes it one of the most popular recreational areas in Florida. Circa 1940s, $3-5.

Hillsborough River State Park. Like many Florida rivers, the water is tea-colored because of the tannic acid carried into it from surrounding swamps. The Hillsborough River probably served as a natural boundary separating the different Indian tribes in the sixteenth century. Circa 1940s, $2-4

Port of Tampa. The Port of Tampa holds a prominent place in Tampa's economic history. The port, which once received such cargo as bananas and was an export center for Florida cattle, is now known mainly for transporting phosphate from Tampa to ports world-wide. Circa 1914, $4-6.

Devil Fish. This view shows a Devil Fish, 12 x 6" long, that was caught in the Tampa Bay. The sender of this card, mailed in Tampa, wrote, "How would you like to catch a fish like that." Cancelled 1912, $5-7.

Port Tampa.
An aerial view of three ships docked at Port Tampa. Cancelled 1954, $2-4.

Tampa's Harbor.
A bird's eye view of Tampa harbor. Cancelled 1920, $3-5.

Riverfront Scene.
A Hillsborough River boat scene taken from the Lafayette Street (now Kennedy Boulevard) Bridge. Shown are three-masted schooners docked along the riverbank. Circa 1908, $5-7.

Boats on the River. This view shows several boats docked in Port Tampa. Circa 1910s, $7-9.

Lafayette Street Bridge. The Lafayette Street (now Kennedy Boulevard) Bridge, constructed in 1913, is one of Tampa's main bridges crossing over Hillsborough River. The Tampa Bay Hotel is shown in the background. Circa 1920s, $3-5.

Plant Park. A view of Plant Park between Tampa Bay Hotel and Hillsborough River. The park was a favorite spot for garden parties in the 1920s. Yachts would dock along the park, so that their passengers could attend functions at the hotel. The Hillsborough River flows by the Tampa Bay Hotel and through the heart of Tampa. Circa 1912, $3-5.

Waterworks on the Hillsborough River. This waterworks plant was built on Hillsborough River to serve the city of Tampa. Circa 1920s, $3-5.

Six Mile Creek. Shown is a bridge over Six Mile Creek, a small waterway flowing into Sparkman Bay (now McKay Bay) about six miles east of downtown Tampa. Circa 1910s, $3-5.

Ballast Point Pavilion. In the late 1800s, the streetcar was the popular mode of travel to this social and recreational center. Shown are people enjoying the facility. The pavilion, miles south of downtown Tampa, burned to the ground in August 1922. Cancelled 1922, $3-5.

Tampa Beaches. The best beaches in the Tampa area are on the Gulf of Mexico; however, Tampa does have some beach space, primarily along Davis Islands, and on the Tampa end of the Davis Causeway (now the Courtney Campbell Parkway). Shown is Palmetto Beach, a picturesque peninsula along the shores of Sparkman Bay (now McKay Bay). Circa 1914, $3-5.

Shrimp Fleet. Many shrimp boats call Tampa home port. The slips on Hooker's Point, not far from downtown Tampa, where the shrimp boats unload, are a favorite stop for tourists. At most times there are about twenty-five boats in port. Circa 1940s, $2-4.

Bird's Eye View. This view shows the Tampa Bay Hotel alongside Hillsborough River. Circa 1920, $1-3.

University of Tampa. An aerial view of Hillsborough River and the campus of the University of Tampa. Circa 1950s, $1-3.

Chapter Six:

Hotels

Tampa Bay Hotel. On February 5, 1891, Henry B. Plant opened the exotic Tampa Bay Hotel, a Moorish fantasy complete with thirteen silver minarets. The hotel, modeled partly after the Alhambra Palace in Granada, Spain, was twelve hundred feet long, five stories high, with five hundred eleven rooms that rented for $30-$75 a day. Circa 1907, $4-6.

Bird's Eye View of the Tampa Bay Hotel. A horse drawn carriage travels on the Lafayette Street (now Kennedy Boulevard) Bridge over Hillsborough River. The Tampa Bay Hotel is shown in the background. Cancelled 1913, $3-5.

Tampa Bay Hotel. The opulent grandeur of the Tampa Bay Hotel was a unique setting for Tampa's social events in the 1920s. Guests came by rail, steamship, and yacht to Henry Plant's huge Moorish castle. They danced to the music of the Boston Symphony musicians, gambled in the casino, and played a new game imported from Scotland—golf. Cancelled 1923, $4-6.

Gardens at Tampa Bay. Henry B. Plant embarked on a massive landscaping project to provide the proper setting for his exclusive resort hotel. The gardens in front of the Tampa Bay Hotel are now known as "Plant Park," named in honor of the man who opened Tampa to development. Circa 1915, $4-6.

Main Entrance. The rooms in the historic Tampa Bay Hotel have hosted truly amazing figures, such as Teddy Roosevelt, Babe Ruth, Clara Barton, and the Queen of England. Circa 1907, $4-6.

Then and Now. Henry B. Plant's Tampa Bay Hotel looks much the same today as it did on its 1891 opening. Moorish stalactites still grace the main entrance. But, instead of guests, the venerable hotel now houses the University of Tampa, and in the west wing, the Henry B. Plant Museum. The massive building is as strong as the bricks in its walls and as delicate as the fine antiques that fill its museum. Circa 1930s, $4-6.

Spar No Expense! Along with many distinctions, Tampa Bay Hotel had Florida's first elevator, a special lighting system designed by Thomas Edison, and delicately-sized telephones made especially for the hotel by Bell Telephone Company. Circa 1907, $4-6.

Hotel and Grounds. Located on Hillsborough River, Tampa Bay Hotel, with its distinguishing minarets, is considered an outstanding example of Moorish-Turkish architecture and was one of the first Tampa structures to be listed in the National Register of Historic Places. Cancelled 1923, $3-5.

Plant's Brass Dogs.
Brought from Europe by Henry B. Plant, Maurice de Nouvilliers' Au Coup de Fusil life-size bronze dogs are located in Plant Park. Circa 1920s, $2-4.

Dining Room. The dining room in the Tampa Bay Hotel. Circa 1915, $2-4.

Hotel Grounds. The park surrounding the Tampa Bay Hotel was as attractive as nature and skilled gardeners could make it. Circa 1920s, $2-4.

DeSoto Oak. The DeSoto Oak tree in Plant Park stands opposite the eastern entrance to Tampa Bay Hotel. Under this tree, legend—but only legend—says that Spanish explorer Hernando De Soto parleyed with the Indians. Underneath the oak is Au Coup de Fusil, a life-size bronze of two dogs pointing for the shot. Circa 1920s, $1-3.

Fountain. The fountain in Plant Park. In the 1920s social events took place in the Tea Gardens around this fountain. Circa 1920s, $1-3.

Plant's Dogs. Plant's dogs were later removed from their original base and relocated in Plant Park. Circa 1970s, $1-3.

Palm Avenue. A peaceful path in Plant Park. Circa 1908, $2-4.

Hotel Statue. "Spinning Girl from the South of France" and a faux tapestry were two of the many treasures brought from Europe by Henry B. Plant to enrich his Tampa Bay Hotel. Circa 1992, $1-3.

DeSoto Hotel. The 150-room DeSoto Hotel was Tampa's principal year-round hotel for two decades. The hotel, built in 1892-93, was designed by James A. Wood, the architect of the Tampa Bay Hotel and the old Hillsborough County Courthouse. The landmark hotel was destroyed in 1949. Cancelled 1913, $8-10.

Alligator Border Postcard. This Alligator Border Postcard illustrates Henry B. Plant's unique Tampa Bay Hotel. It is the most distinctive landmark in Tampa. Horseshoe arches and Byzantine silver domes combine with the Moorish minarets to give the hotel a look like none other. Circa 1915, $40-45.

Hotel Floridan. Tampa's tallest building for several decades was the eighteen-story Hotel Floridan, which had been built during the land boom of the 1920s. Circa 1920s, $4-6.

Veranda. The verandas at Tampa Bay Hotel are of great length and width and were often filled with happy guests. Circa 1915, $40-45.

Hillsboro Hotel. The Hillsboro Hotel opened in 1912 and served travelers to Tampa for more than half a century. Located on Florida Avenue between Madison and Twiggs streets, the hotel had an unexcelled dining room known as the "Top of the Town." In 1946, a single room with bath at the Hillsboro cost $3. Cancelled 1916, $5-7.

Hillsboro Hotel. The Hillsboro was the largest all-year hotel in Tampa. Circa 1907, $5-7.

Bay View Hotel. Shown is the 125-room Bay View Hotel on Washington Street near Franklin Street when it was a popular hostelry. The ten-story hotel was built in 1912. In February 1980 the Bay View Hotel was imploded to make room for a new Tampa skyscraper building. Cancelled 1927, $5-7.

Tampa Terrace Hotel. A 1925 view of the Tampa Terrace Hotel that was built next to the 1891 Hillsborough County Courthouse. This was Tampa's most elegant establishment between 1926 and 1965. Circa 1920s, $4-6.

Bay Shore Royal Hotel. Circa 1930s, $3-5.

Mirasol Hotel and Yacht Basin.
Another boom time hotel in Tampa was the Mirasol Hotel. Circa 1920s, $3-5.

Chapter Seven:

Clubs

Elks Club.
The 1905 Elks Club, at Florida Avenue and Madison Street, once a private wood-frame house, was located opposite the Hillsborough County Courthouse in downtown Tampa. In 1913 it was replaced with a red-brick building. Circa 1910s, $2-4.

Elks Home. **For decades, one of the attractive landmarks in the heart of downtown Tampa was the elegant red brick building of the Elks Lodge at the corner of Florida Avenue and Madison Street. The structure was erected in 1913. Circa 1920s, $2-4.**

Tampa Yacht Club. Circa 1950s, $1-3.

Tampa Yacht and Country Club. The Tampa Yacht and Country Club, located on Bayshore Boulevard on Tampa Bay, is one of the oldest social clubs in Tampa. The top part of the card is a water view; the bottom part a land view. Cancelled 1919, $2-4.

Davis Islands Country Club. A view of the Country Club on Davis Islands, a community in downtown Tampa. This exclusive development also offered, among other amenities, a coliseum, canals, and yacht basin. It called itself "The Eighth Wonder Of The World." Circa 1920s, $2-4.

Temple Terrace Country Club. Circa 1920s, $2-4.

Chapter Eight:
Churches

The Rock Church. **The Episcopal House of Prayer, known as the "Rock Church," was built entirely of Florida rock. This quaint little church at the corner of Michigan and Central avenues was considered one of the most unusual and attractive structures of its kind in the South. It was constructed of flint rock taken from the bed of Hillsborough River within a few miles of Tampa. When designing the church, L. A. Fort used a style of architecture that was commonly practiced during the early centuries of Christianity in the British Isles. Circa 1920s, $3-5.**

First Baptist Church. **The First Baptist Church on Kennedy Boulevard, across from the University of Tampa, began in 1859 and established its present site in the early 1920s. Circa 1930s, $3-5.**

Convent of the Holy Name. The establishment of the Roman Catholic Church comprises, beside its handsome church edifices, the Convent of the Holy Name, a high school in charge of the Sisters of the Holy Name. Built in 1907, this three-story brick school had eighteen nuns as teachers. Circa 1910s, $4-6.

First Methodist Church. The First Methodist Church, a landmark in downtown Tampa for years, has founding dates back to 1851. Stonewall Jackson reportedly contributed $5 toward the original church building. This structure was demolished in the late 1960s. Circa 1910, $4-6.

Hyde Park Methodist Church.
The Hyde Park Methodist Church, built in 1907, is located at the corner of Platt Street and Cedar Avenue. Cancelled 1912, $3-5.

First Christian Church. Circa 1930s, $3-5.

Church of the Sacred Heart.
This beautiful Roman Catholic church, built in 1905, is located in downtown Tampa at the southeast corner of Twiggs Street and Florida Avenue. Distinguishing features are its marble front, Munich windows and costly fittings. A huge arched loggia takes up two-thirds of the front. Circa 1910, $4-6.

Chapter Nine:

Sulphur Springs

Sulphur Springs, located on Hillsborough River just north of downtown Tampa, was a popular community and recreational area throughout the early 1900s. In 1900, Dr. J.H. Mills opened the Sulphur Springs recreational area that included a swimming pool, a dance pavilion, a Ferris wheel, a toboggan water slide, a high diving platform and an arcade. The popular facility was Tampa's version of Coney Island. Until the trolley line ran to the site in 1908, the springs could only be reached by bicycle or horse and buggy across a wooden bridge. This mammoth spring flowed 60,000 gallons of water per minute and had a constant temperature of seventy-two degrees. In 1927 a picturesque water tower was built; it became a major Tampa landmark. The tower top had a tank that held 200,000 gallons of water, supplied by a spring at the base of the tower.

During the early 1900s, Sulphur Springs conducted most of its business in one arcade building. An apartment hotel occupied the upper floor; on the ground floor were a post office, a café, a barbershop, a beauty parlor, a bank, and several stores. The Sulphur Springs' Greyhound Track provided residents and tourists with racing entertainment from December to April. Sulphur Springs rapidly became the sport and athletic center of all Florida and eventually became part of Tampa in 1923.

***Sulphur Springs Swimming Pool*. Above Tampa, on Hillsborough River, a popular natural water attraction was opened to the public by Dr. J. H. Mills in 1900. Before 1908, when a trolley line ran to the site, the springs could be reached only by horse and buggy or bicycle over a narrow rickety bridge. This mammoth springs flowed 60,000 gallons of water per minute. Shown are people enjoying the springs. Circa 1908, $12-14.**

***Before Commercialization*. This is how Sulphur Springs looked in the 1890s before being commercialized. At that time it was a popular swimming hole. Cancelled 1906, $12-14.**

Entrance to Sulphur Springs.
A wooden bridge led to the entrance of Sulphur Springs. Cancelled 1913, $3-5

Picnic Grounds and Bridge. This view shows the picnic grounds at one end of the wooden bridge that led to Sulphur Springs. Circa 1908, $8-10.

Early Morning View. A view of the Springs without people. Cancelled 1908, $8-10.

Hillsborough River Scene.
The Sulphur Springs shoreline on Hillsborough River. Circa 1910, $4-6.

One of America's Wonders. Shown is a typical scene at Sulphur Springs Swimming Pool. It became one of the most popular recreation centers in Florida. Circa 1915, $5-7.

Swimming Pool. The Sulphur Springs pool was open all year with a 25-cent admission fee. The pool had an average temperature of seventy-two degrees. Circa 1910, $8-10.

Look Out Below. This view shows a brave fellow diving from the high platform into the Sulphur Springs pool. Cancelled 1922, $5-7.

Toboggan Water Slide. In the early 1900s, Sulphur Springs was sought out not only for the restorative powers of its waters, but also for the pool, Ferris wheel, dance pavilion, and arcade. Sulphur Springs was dubbed "Tampa's answer to Coney Island." Shown are participants and observers at the Toboggan Water Slide. Cancelled 1927, $5-7.

Sulphur Springs Water Tower.
This imposing tower, built in 1927, is one of Tampa's best land and aerial marks. The top has a tank that once held 200,000 gallons of pure water supplied by a spring in the base of the tower. The tower is still standing and can be seen when driving on Interstate 275 in Tampa. Circa 1930s, $4-6.

Beach and Pool.
Swimmers playing on a platform in the Sulphur Springs pool. Circa 1930s, $3-5.

Business Street Scene.
A business street scene at Sulphur Springs. The Sulphur Spring was a popular recreational facility for many years. Later, the area was incorporated as part of Tampa. The Sulphur Springs Arcade Building is shown on the left. Circa 1930s, $8-10.

Sulphur Springs Greyhound Track.
During the 1930s, the dog track at Sulphur Springs was open from December to April. This dog track eventually became the Tampa Greyhound Track. Circa 1930s, $10-12.

Sulphur Springs Alligator Card. A Sulphur Springs scene is illustrated on this Alligator Border postcard. The Alligator Border Series, published by Langsdorf, is in great demand with postcard collectors. Circa 1910, $40-45.

Chapter Ten:

Ybor City

More than one hundred years ago, Tampa's Board of Trade persuaded Vicente Martinez Ybor to move his cigar-making business from Key West to Tampa. Ybor City's first cigar was produced in 1886, and the community soon grew to become the biggest cigar-manufacturing center in the world. Ybor City was home to more than 20,000 Cuban, Spanish and Italian immigrants who worked in the cigar factories and brought to Tampa the Latin influence it retains today. The immigrants developed their own hospitals, clubhouses, theaters and businesses.

With the advent of the Spanish-American War, Tampa became a focal point for media attention. Colonel Theodore Roosevelt encamped his volunteer cavalry unit, the Rough Riders, at Port Tampa. While Ybor City was off limits to his soldiers, Colonel Roosevelt took parties of officers, newspaper reporters, and visiting dignitaries to the Hotel El Pasaje there for long dinner parties. El Pasaje also entertained a famous Spanish-American War correspondent, Richard Harding Davis, artist Frederick Remington, and later Winston Churchill came here as a correspondent. Many other big names have dined and wined at the famous Ybor City restaurant, including President Grover Cleveland, many Florida governors, Cuban President Grau San Martin and the famous actress, Lupe Velez.

By 1900, Ybor City and West Tampa were diverse communities of Cuban, Spanish, Italian, Jewish, and German immigrants. A unique heritage was created when the various cultures were intermixed and natives knew how to speak several languages, with Spanish being the most predominant. The blending of these heritages created a new one.

In the early 1900s, another group of European immigrants, Sicilians, relocated to Ybor City and settled on the outskirts of the thriving community that was then called Pachata. Unofficially banned from working in the cigar factories, Sicilians sought their livelihood in agriculture. In time they came to dominate the produce and dairy businesses. Later, when they had learned Spanish, they were admitted to the cigar facto ries.

The community flourished until World War II as machines continued to replace workers in the cigar factories and young Latins moved to the suburbs. In the 1960s, an Urban Renewal project demolished more than six hundred homes and businesses, but replaced few of them. The Ybor City of today has half-empty blocks and vacant storefronts interspersed with historic landmarks and family-owned businesses. The historic Columbia Restaurant and Ybor Square, a collection of shops and restaurants in Tampa's first cigar factory, are Ybor City's biggest draws. The heart of the district is La Septima (Seventh Avenue), a hot spot at night, mobbed with crowds enjoying the strains of music escaping from its nightclubs and the intoxicating aroma of Cuban coffee. The area's cigar-making history can be found in the Ybor City State Museum.

Greetings from Ybor City.
Ybor City was named a National Historic Landmark District because of its importance to immigrant, racial, and ethnic history. It has been home to Spaniards, African-Cubans, Cubans, Germans, and Italians and is distinguished by its large number of cigar factories, worker houses, and ethnic clubs that date back to the first two decades of the twentieth century. Many of the red brick buildings that housed the city's cigar industry still stand. Circa 1930s, $4-6.

Spanish Club. The El Centro Espanol on the Ybor Plaza at Seventh Avenue and 16th Street was one of the most active clubhouses in Ybor City. Founded in 1891, it had 2,000 members. This red brick building with an ornate iron grill work balcony over the entrance was built in 1912. It contained a restaurant, a coffee shop, a theater, and was associated with a hospital. Many concerts and balls were held in this structure. Circa 1915, $8-10.

Cigar Factories. Following unrest in Cuba in the 1880s, many Cubans followed Vincent Martinez Ybor to the promise of a new life in Florida. Ybor set up a cigar factory first in Key West and later in what would become Ybor City in Tampa. Rows of workers meticulously hand-rolled Havana cigars in Ybor's factory while the lector, a reader who was located in an elevated area above the workers, read from newspapers, magazines, and novels of the day. In the 1920s, more than 13,000 people were employed in Tampa's 125 cigar factories. This view shows a busy scene in a Ybor City cigar factory. In 1925, over a thousand cigar makers were at work in this room. Many of the red brick cigar factory buildings remain relatively unchanged. Today, however, most of these buildings have been converted to other uses. Circa 1920s, $5-7.

Seventh Avenue Street Scene. A view looking east on Seventh Avenue, Ybor City's main street. To the visitor Ybor City offers an old world charm and hospitality, a fascinating, colorful Latin atmosphere in modern surroundings. Circa 1915, $12-14.

Seventh Avenue Scene. This Seventh Avenue street scene shows the El Centro Espanol, an Ybor City clubhouse on the right. Circa 1915, $4-6.

Senoritas in Ybor City.
Beautiful Latin ladies posed on the steps of Centro Asturiano during La Verbena del Tobaco—a fiesta promoted by the Tampa Cigar Manufacturing Association. Circa 1930s, $5-7.

Serenading in Ybor City.
Festivals and fiestas brought costumed residents into the streets, providing a field day for photographers. Popular fiestas were the Spanish Bean Soup Festival and the Latin American Fiesta. Circa 1930s, $2-4

Colorful Costumes.
A beautiful senorita dressed in a colorful Spanish costume is admired by a handsome caballero, as she strolls through Ybor City, the picturesque Latin Quarter of Tampa. Here one can enjoy the atmosphere of old Madrid as they visit the historical sites and dine in the famous restaurants with authentic Spanish cuisine. Circa 1940s, $1-3.

***Spanish Ladies*. Two beautiful senoritas in colorful Spanish costumes during an Ybor City fiesta. Circa 1940, $3-5.**

City Scene. An "untouristed" Latin flavor accents Tampa's Latin Quarter. On the streets, and in the restaurants and clubs, are heard the cadences of a Latin language; movies, theaters and concerts are performed in Spanish. Many of the buildings represent Cuban and Spanish architecture and relate primarily to the cigar industry that brought the area to life in the late nineteenth century. Circa 1940s, $2-4.

Cascaden Park. During the hot Florida summer months, many people of Ybor City hung out at the swimming pool in Cascaden Park. Circa 1940s, $2-4.

Cuban Bread. When Juan More came to Tampa, he carried in his pocket a piece of paper that held his own recipe for making Cuban bread. In Tampa, he introduced his own special formula of Pan-Cubano, and its popularity has endured to this day. Cuban bread is like no other loaf in the world. It is leavened with emotion, flavored with tradition, and eaten with a large helping of nostalgia. Circa 1950s, $3-5.

Chapter Eleven:

Gasparilla Celebration

In the late 1700s and early 1800s, the waters sur rounding Florida were filled with brigantines, slave ships, bootleggers, merchants and frigates from Spain, England, and the young United States... and pirates. The pirates were an early version of today's organized crime—with leaders, a strict code of honor, and their own form of government.

Legend has it that Pirate Jose Gaspar, better known as Gasparilla, reined in the Florida Keys and along Florida's west coast from Marco Island to Tampa Bay. The barrier islands along Florida's Gulf Coast, the rivers, and harbors were a perfect location for international outlaws to establish a base of operations.

The Annual Pirate Invasion

Tampa's main social event occurs each year in February when the dread pirate, Jose Gaspar, seizes the helpless city, subjecting its citizens to his whims. The Gasparilla Festival, named for the pirate Jose Gaspar, "last of the Buccaneers," now rivals New Orleans' Mardi Gras and Miami's Orange Bowl festivals as one of the largest outpourings of merrymaking in the land. The festival, led by an "invasion" of pirates, features parades, swank society parties, revelry in Ybor City, fireworks, dances, and, in general, a celebration of the ending of the "grueling" two-month winter. Although the Gasparilla festivities go all the way back to 1904, the real story of the city's favorite pirate, Jose Gaspar, goes back much farther, to the waning days of the Spanish Main.

***High Carnival under the Skull and Bones!* The only city in the world that is certain to be invaded and captured by pirates every February. Tampa turns surrender into a week of high carnival that annually attracts some of Florida's largest crowds. A postcard booklet. Circa 1940s, $8-10.**

Tampa's Own Buccaneer

Jose Gaspar was born near Seville, Spain in 1756. Gaspar began his career as a lieutenant in the Royal Spanish Navy. In 1783, while serving on the Florida Blanca, Gaspar and his compatriot, Roderigo Lopez, led a bloody mutiny, captured the ship, and headed for the Florida Straits to set up business as pirates. During this journey, Gaspar changed his name to "Gasparilla." After reaching Florida, Gasparilla sailed up the west coast, set up headquarters on one of the islands, and named it Gasparilla Island.

During the following twelve years, Gaspar looted and sunk thirty-six ships. Gaspar quickly became known as something of a local Bluebeard, and stories of his bloody raids struck a note of fear in both Spanish and American merchantmen.

Gaspar and his merry band of buccaneers dominated west Florida's coastal waters during the lat e eighteenth and early nineteenth century. The legendary pirate was a paradox of good breeding and low morals, prone both to bloodthirsty acts and surprising kindnesses.

Gaspar continued his pirating career for forty years. His downfall came in 1821, when he attempted to capture a United States warship, the *U.S.S. Enterprise*, in disguise. The quick-moving battle left Gaspar's ship a burning wreck. It is rumored that rather than surrendering, Jose Gaspar wrapped himself in chains and jumped into the sea.

Birth of the Festival

The Gasparilla Festival was started in 1904 by Louise Dodge, society editor of the Tampa Tribune, who was trying to enliven a May festival she was planning. It was suggested to her by George W. Hardee that Tampa have an invasion by the pirate Gasparilla. Tampa's annual Gasparilla Carnival stated with the first invasion on May 4, 1904. The Gasparilla event has been continuous except for 1907, 1908, 1909, and the World War I and II years. Today, the Gasparilla Festival is held in February concurrently with the Florida State Fair. Each year, a king and queen are crowned to reign over the pirate crew. The Gasparilla Festival traditionally winds up with a night parade through Ybor City, that still-living creation of cigar king Vicente Martinez Ybor.

Early Parades

The first Gasparilla Festival was a complete success, except for the pirates, who, as part of the Flower Parade, invaded Tampa on horseback. In 1905, there was a triumphant celebration as all sixty automobiles in Tampa rolled in the parade. In 1911, for the first time, the pirate invasion came by ship, which sailed up Hillsborough River with roaring cannons, proudly flying the Jolly Roger. The pirate ship, *Jose Gasparilla,* was constructed of steel in a shipyard in 1953. It is a 165-foot long, three-mast replica of a West Indiaman typical of the type commandeered and used by pirates in Gaspar's day. It is the only working pirate ship in the world. It resides at its dockside Tampa birth behind Curtis Hixon Hall year round except for the time it is used in the annual invasion.

Annual Invasion of Tampa By Gasparilla Pirates.
The Gasparilla tradition dates back to 1904 when a society columnist created a carnival based on the legendary pirate Jose Gaspar. The festival includes a ball, invasion brunch, pirate invasion, parade and downtown street party. Shown is the 165-foot black-hulled Jose Gasparilla, escorted by a flotilla of boats, during the Gasparilla invasion. Circa 1930s, $2-4.

Gasparilla Carnival.
The sender of this card said, "I stood on this new bridge to watch the landing of the pirate ship. It was great." Cancelled 1915, $8-10.

Gasparilla Pirate Festival.
Gasparilla Week opens with a full-scale invasion of Tampa by the Pirates of Ye Mystic Krewe of Gasparilla who sails into Tampa's harbor aboard their colorful three-masted sloop-of-war, the corsair *Jose Gasparilla*. To the booming of cannon and the rattle of small arms, the ship forces its way through the city's bridges and the swashbucklng pirate crew lands. A spectacular pirate parade then winds its way in triumph through the streets, with beautiful floats and bands in the line of march. The rest of the week is a succession of gala events—night parades and street dancing in Tampa's Latin Quarter; a Coronation Ball for the newly chosen Pirate King; a Children's Pirate Parade; and finally, the departure of the pirate ship at night against a backdrop of brilliant fireworks. Circa 1940s, S2-4.

Parade on Franklin Street. Tampa has adopted Jose Gaspar (also known as Gasparilla) as its patron rogue. The annual Gasparilla Carnival induces staid citizens to dress like pirates and participate in the carnival. Shown are floats in Tampa's Gasparilla Celebration parading down Franklin Street in an elevated view. Circa 1930s, $3-5.

Parade Route. The 3.5 mile long Gasparilla Parade begins two miles south of downtown Tampa on scenic Bayshore Boulevard and winds along Hillsborough Bay into downtown—to the delight of several hundred thousand festival onlookers from around Tampa Bay and across the region. Circa 1930s, $3-5.

Children's Pirate Parade. The Children's Gasparilla Parade, a part of Tampa's Gasparilla celebration since 1947, is scheduled one week before the pirate invasion and the main Gasparilla Parade. Both parades follow the same route along Bayshore Boulevard. The Children's Parade ends with a spectacular fireworks display as an imaginary "piratechnic" sea battle takes place over Hillsborough Bay, setting the stage for a smooth and festive invasion of Tampa on the following Saturday. Circa 1930s, $3-5.

Gasparilla Festival Brochure. This brochure describes the event. It's high noon in Tampa Monday, February 10, 1958! A full-rigged pirate ship comes blasting its way into the harbor, rocked by the thunders of its own broadsides, its decks swarming with jack-booted buccaneers. Cutlasses flash in the warm Florida sun. A scene out of the eighteenth century—a pirate invasion that, if it were for keeps, would "shiver your timbers!" But it's only lively, gorgeous make believe—a rollicking reenactment of happenings out of Tampa's storied past, staged by the modern Pirates of Gasparilla, who thus play yo-ho-ho with history. And they have played it—to the hilt—annually since 1904. Circa 1958, $10-12.

Friendly Invasion. Escorted by a flotilla of many boats, the Jose Gasparilla flies only flags of fun as it pulls into Harbour Island during the Gasparilla invasion of Tampa. Circa 1940s, $3-5.

Gasparilla Festival/Florida State Fair. Tampa's Gasparilla Celebration is held each February concurrently with the Florida State Fair. Circa 1940s, $8-10.

Chapter Twelve:

Leisure Activities

Let's Go Canoeing. A canoeing party on Hillsborough River just above Sulphur Springs reflected America's growing passion for outdoor recreation. These couples seem to be enjoying the tranquility and romantic setting of the river. Circa 1917, $4-6.

Tampa Alligator Farm. This postcard from the Tampa Alligator Farm in Sulphur Springs shows one of the boarders scooting down the slide and splashing into the alligator pool. This isn't a trick. The alligator is simply trying to get away from a handler at the rear of the slide who urges him onward. Circa 1920s, $6-8.

Fishing. Tropical climate and abundant sea life in the waters near Tampa make fishing a very popular activity. Shown is the fish caught in a one-day fishing trip. Circa 1920s, $3-5.

Municipal Band Shell. This view shows a typical gathering of tourists to hear concerts rendered by national and local bands during the winter season. Cancelled 1931, $1-3.

Tampa Theater. The lavish Tampa Theater opened in 1926, joining the ranks of the great American atmospheric movie "palaces." Designed by renowned theater architect John Eberson, it boasted clouds floating across a domed ceiling, a mighty Wurlitzer organ, and air conditioning. The theater was housed in an ornate, ten-story building that became one of the city's most impressive landmarks. Its decor blended Greek Revival, Italian Renaissance, and Mediterranean exotic styles. Today, movie-goers marvel at the ornate interior of the theater, which recreates the courtyard of an Italian villa. Before shows, musicians treated patrons to the sounds of the theater's 868-pipe organ. Circa 1920s, $4-6.

Alligators. A person in Tampa sent this alligator card to a friend in New York City. The postcard illustrates that the alligator's pace is leisurely. Most of the time it is in no hurry to do anything. Cancelled 1925, $4-6.

Sunshine Park.
Opened in 1926, in 1947 the Tampa Downs thoroughbred horse racing track was renamed Sunshine Park and hosted its inaugural meet. The track had 650 horse stalls, an official tote board, an electric starting gate, and a photo finish camera. Legendary sportswriter Grantland Rice coined the phrase "Santa Anita of the South" in his many columns when referring to this facility. In 1980 the track was renamed Tampa Bay Downs. Circa 1948, $4-6.

Speedboat Races.
In a city ringed by marinas and backyard docks, there were many water sports including power boating as shown in this postcard. Records fell with almost each meet as the waterways around Tampa offered speed lanes to high-powered motor boats. Cancelled 1933, $4-6.

Bird's Eye View of Fair Grounds.
As one of the four largest expositions in America, the Florida State Fair, held in Tampa during February each year, was recognized as the world's greatest winter carnival. Annually, it attracted thousands of visitors from every section of the nation. Combined with the wealth of agricultural and industrial displays that filled twenty-five mammoth fire-proof exhibition halls and over 365,000 square feet of floor space, the Florida State Fair annually presented the current featured attractions available to the show world. Originally located in the center of Tampa, adjoining the beautiful campus of the University of Tampa (formerly the Tampa Bay Hotel), the fair grounds included the Fair buildings, race track, grandstand, and other public facilities. Later the Fair Grounds were relocated to another area in Tampa. Cancelled 1948, $8-10.

Auto Races.
Shown are the auto races held on the Florida State Race Track at the Fair Grounds. Circa 1940s, $8-10.

Let's Go to the Fair!
Crowds jam to get into the entrance of the Florida State Fair in this postcard view. The Fair, held each February, is the show window of the state and one of the largest winter expositions in the world. Circa 1940s, $8-10.

Moss-Festooned Lagoon at Dupree Gardens. Dupree Gardens, located seventeen miles north of Tampa, was a vast fairyland with flowers everywhere—millions upon millions of blossoms tucked into shaded nooks, along winding pathways, in artistically arranged beds. Rustic bridges, quiet pools, the tinkling sound of a waterfall, and soft music coming from singing birdhouses in the trees lent enchantment to the scene. This attraction was open during the years 1940-1954. Circa 1940s, $4-6.

Dupree Gardens Brochure. The *Tampa Daily Times* reported, "Those who have visited Dupree Gardens went away ready to boost them to their friends and to put a visit high up on the 'must' list when visitors come to town to be shown around. The place is a horticultural paradise right here at home." Circa 1940s, $6-8.

Mirror Pool in Dupree Gardens.
In 1946 the admittance fee was $1 to visit Dupree Gardens, a nationally known attraction that had acres of beautiful flowering trees, shrubs, and annuals bordering winding pathways and tinkling streams, all literally set to the music of the Old Masters. Circa 1940s, $4-6.

Fun You Can Bet On. Jai-Alai, developed in the 1600s in the Basque area of France and Spain, is one of the world's most dangerous sports and one of the oldest ball games known. It is played with a rock-hard ball that is propelled at speeds up to 150 miles per hour. The game, first watched in Miami in 1926, was played in several Jai Alai arenas including the Tampa Jai-Alai Fronton. The Tampa Fronton, opened in 1953, later became part of the Florida Gaming Corporation and closed in 1998. Circa 1950s, $4-6.

Jai Alai Players.
Jai Alai is similar to super-fast handball, played with a basket-like arm extension called a "cesta" to accelerate the speed and accuracy of the ball. Velocity and skillful handling of the ball require all players on the floor to be in constant motion. Circa 1950s, $4-6.

Busch Gardens. In the 1960s Busch Gardens was the most popular free attraction in Florida. Later, the Busch family added an African plain complete with animals, a number of sanitized versions of foreign locations, an amusement park, and an admission charge. Busch Gardens, which was the first of Florida's major modern theme parks, started out modestly in 1959. Circa 1960s, $1-3.

Tampa Greyhound Track. During the 1930s the Sulphur Springs Greyhound Track provided Tampa residents and visitors with racing entertainment from December to April. This track eventually became the Tampa Greyhound Track. Circa 1960s, $1-3.

Greyhound Racing.
Normally, eight dogs compete in each race. The dogs are released from numbered "traps" in pursuit of an electrically controlled and propelled mechanical hare. One of the great attractions of dog racing is that it can be seen by fans from the start to finish. The racing oval is only about ¼ mile. Circa 1960s, $1-3.

Anheuser Busch Brewery.
A striking view of the Anheuser Busch Brewery. The stairway to the stars—one of the world's longestescalators, and the beautiful Hospitality House, located at Busch Gardens. Circa 1960s, $1-3.

Skyrail Safari. Busch Gardens Skyrail Safari arriving at the Monorail Station after a trip over the African Veldt. The Clock Tower of the Old Swiss House and the surface train are visible in the background. Circa 1960s, $1-3

Chapter Thirteen:

Potpourri

Celery Field. Florida agriculture employs more workers and produces more money value than any other basic industry; in fact, it ranks second only to the tourist industry. Long trains of refrigerated cars moving swiftly along railroads to northern markets and large numbers of rumbling trucks rolling along the highways filled with oranges, grapefruit, tomatoes, celery, potatoes and other vegetables represent an important business in Florida. Trainloads of sugar, paper-shell pecans, tropical fruits, and strawberries all help to swell Florida's income. Shown in this postcard is a celery field in Tampa. Cancelled 1910, $2-4.

Picking Oranges. Citrus groves thrive in the Tampa area. Shown are workers harvesting a large orange crop. Hand picking "Florida gold," the citrus that forms a large part of the sunshine state's agricultural activity. Throughout the years, Hillsborough County citrus groves have produced hundreds of thousands of crates of citrus each year for the markets of the nation. Circa 1930, $3-5.

Fruit Exhibit.
Citrus exhibit at the Florida State Fair in Tampa. Circa 1930s, $1-3.

Citrus Processing. The processing of citrus products is one of Florida's most important industries. Fresh fruit, citrus concentrate, and canned citrus segments are but a few of the products produced by Florida's citrus businesses. Shown in this Tampa processing plant are workers preparing grapefruit for canning. Circa 1920s, $3-5.

Citrus Grove.
Shown is a citrus grove in the Tampa area. Visitors to Florida should visit a grove so that they will understand why citrus trees were considered ornamental, grown to grace the imperial gardens of ancient Oriental rulers long before anyone thought of eating the fruit. Circa 1920s, $2-4.

Citrus Labels. When citrus labels were created in the 1880s, their intent was to leave an impression so the citrus buyer would remember to order that particular brand of fruit again. The colorful fruit crate label was pasted upon the ends of wooden fruit crates. These labels were from citrus groves in the Tampa area. Shown are 1930s citrus labels that were reproduced as postcards. The original labels, which are very valuable, are prized by collectors. Circa 1980s, $1-3.

University of Tampa. The University of Tampa receives accolades as a well-respected liberal arts school with an international student body. The university maintains as its first duty an experienced and highly qualified faculty and offers instruction in almost every branch of science. Circa 1930s, $2-4.

University of Tampa. The minarets of the University of Tampa provide a visible landmark of Tampa's heritage. The university's main building was originally the Tampa Bay Hotel that had been built by railroad magnate Henry B. Plant in 1891. Circa 1930s, $2-4.

Plant Park. Even before Henry B. Plant started his hotel empire, he began to beautify his grounds with flowers, shrubs, and trees. An old catalog of plantings listed more than 150 varieties on the hotel grounds. Included were twenty kinds of palm trees, thirteen ferns, nine kinds of cacti, three types of bananas, and twelve kinds of orchids and citrus trees. Cancelled 1939, $2-4.

Greetings From MacDill Field.
Tampa's U.S. Army Air Base "MacDill Field" was an important military base during World War II. The base was later renamed MacDill Air Force Base. Circa 1930s, $3-5.

MacDill Air Force Base.
In 1942, young American pilots began training on B-26 medium bombers at MacDill. Many of the pilots trained at MacDill were stationed in Europe during World War II. Circa 1940s, $4-6.

Drew Field/Tampa Airport.
In 1939, the city of Tampa leased Drew Field to the Army, which turned Drew Field into a military facility with improved runways. This was an important World War II facility. For a while after World War II, Tampa's International Airport operated out of deserted barracks buildings at Drew Field. On August 17, 1952 a new terminal was opened at Tampa International Airport. Shown is the Officers' Club at Drew Field. Circa 1940s, $2-4.

Greetings from Drew Field.
Drew Field was an important airfield during World War II. In 1947 it was converted into the Tampa International Airport, which became one of Florida's major hubs of travel. Circa 1940s, $3-5.

Seminole Culture Center.
The Great Chickee Gift Shop on Orient Road in Tampa houses arts and crafts produced by Seminole Indian artisans from all Florida Indian reservations. Associated with this center was a typical Seminole Indian Village. In 2004 the Seminole Indian tribe opened the Seminole Hard Rock Hotel & Casino just a short distance from this center. Circa 1960s, $1-3.

Chapter Fourteen:

Near Tampa

Many interesting cities and towns surround Tampa. Across Tampa Bay to the west are Clearwater and St. Petersburg. These cities are briefly described in chapters fifteen and sixteen. Other cities in the Tampa area include Arcadia, Bartow, Dunedin, Lakeland, Oldsmar, Plant City, Ruskin, Safety Harbor, St. Leo, Tarpon Springs, Weeki Wachee, Winter Haven, and Zephyrhills.

Arcadia

Arcadia, the county seat and largest city of De Soto County, is located southeast of Tampa. Situated near the beautiful Peace River, the city has cattle ranches, citrus groves, and phosphate strip mines. Rev. James Hendry, who built a sawmill here in 1884, named the town. Rev. Hendry named the town in honor of Arcadia Albritton, who was the daughter of pioneer settlers who had baked him a cake for his birthday. He appreciated it so much he named the city after her.

***Arcadia*. Residents posing for a photo on Oak Street. Circa 1915, $14-16.**

***Arcadia*. The DeSoto County Courthouse, located in Arcadia, was built in 1912 for $75,000. In 1976 the building was restored as a Bicentennial Project. Circa 1920s, $4-6.**

***DeSoto Hotel in Arcadia*. Two of Arcadia's oldest hotels were the Arcadia House built before 1901 and the DeSoto Hotel at the corner of Oak Street and DeSoto Avenue, built about 1904. The DeSoto Hotel was located over the DeSoto National Bank. The lobby and dining room were on the second floor and balconies faced on both streets. Private rooms were on the second and third floors. In 1980 the site was turned into a parking lot. Circa 1915, $8-10.**

Bartow

Bartow, a relaxing city of oak shade trees, is an important phosphate, citrus and cattle center. Located east of Tampa, the phosphate mines here produce eighty percent of the pebble phosphate in the U.S. Raw, ugly pits of the mines can be seen here. This Polk County city was first named Peas Creek, then Fort Blount and, in 1867, the name was changed to honor Confederate General Francis Bartow.

***Bartow*. Conrad Schuck's Wonder House in Bartow. The house is packed full of unique ideas and step saving devices. Beautiful hand-laid tile work and landscaping add much interest to the building. Circa 1930s, $1-3.**

***Bartow*. The Polk County Courthouse, built in 1909-1911, served until a new courthouse was erected in 1987. Circa 1960s, $6-8.**

***Bartow*. The city water works in Bartow. Circa 1930, $6-8.**

***Bartow*. The Methodist Church in Bartow. Circa 1910, $4-6.**

Dunedin

Dunedin is located west of Tampa in Pinellas County. Its early settlers were Scottish, and the community has maintained this heritage. Caladesi Island State Park lies just offshore between Dunedin Beach and Clearwater Beach. The park beach is one of the most beautiful beaches in Florida. Dunedin was established in the late 1860s, and at first was called Jonesboro. The name changed in 1878 when the Scottish settlers arrived.

***Dunedin*. The public dock in Dunedin, on the Gulf of Mexico. Cancelled 1914, $7-9.**

***Dunedin*.**
Bay Shore Drive in Dunedin. Cancelled 1910, $8-10.

Homosassa Springs

A huge spring that flows at a rate of 70,000 gallons a minute is the chief source of water for the short Homosassa River, which empties into the Gulf of Mexico only nine miles to the west. Located north of Tampa, the springs are regarded as curious among naturalists because both fresh and salt-water fish seem equally at home in it. A few miles from the springs are the ruins of the great sugar plantation of Senator David Yulee, which was a prosperous concern before Union soldiers destroyed it during the Civil War.

***Homosassa Springs Alligators*.**
More than fifty alligators and crocodiles bask in the sun or thrash wildly about in the water in pursuit of tossed food at the Gator Lagoon of Homosassa Springs. Circa 1950s, $1-3.

Scenic Boat Ride. **Comfortable deck boats took visitors down scenic waterways at Homosassa Springs. Circa 1950, $1-3**

Gator Lagoon at Homosassa Springs. **Alligators leap high for the bait, to the amusement of a lovely lady, at the Gator Lagoon of Homosassa Springs, located northwest of Tampa. Feeding time is a photographer's delight as the scaly reptiles actually leap for their dinner. Circa 1950s, $1-3.**

Lakeland

Lakeland, located a few miles northeast of Tampa, was incorporated as a city on January 1, 1885. With the town nicely laid out with a park in the center and liberal provision for streets and alleys, it grew rapidly. The city had a railroad station, a drug store, the Tremont Hotel, a bank, a citrus nursery, several general stores and churches for various religious denominations. In 1888 the strawberry industry was established. By 1894 Lakeland was shipping more strawberries than any other place in the state. The Lakeland Light and Power Company erected a light plant at the corner of Cedar Street and Massachusetts Avenue early in 1891. In 1893 twenty trains a day were arriving at and departing from Lakeland's depot. 1895 is known as the year of the "Big Freeze," and Lakeland citizens, like those of other sections of the state, suffered heavy losses. A temperature of eighteen degrees, the coldest South Florida had ever known, was experienced December 27, 1894. Oranges and other citrus fruits were frozen, and many trees were killed. During the night of February 7, 1895, the temperatures again went below twenty degrees and remained below or near freezing until February 10. Nearly all the groves in the state were destroyed, the trees being killed to the ground. In 1896 a cigar factory was built. In May 1898, six thousand troops were quartered in Lakeland, awaiting embarkation for Cuba from Tampa during the Spanish-American War. A large lumber and shingle mill was built and in operation by 1900. A new City Hall, the ACL freight depot and the Hotel Kibler were built in 1913. Business streets were paved with brick and some residential streets were paved with asphalt in 1913. In 1916 the Morrell Memorial Hospital opened for service. In 1917 a brick post office building was erected. Lakeland's first golf course also opened in 1917. In 1922 the Florida Southern College began the first semester of the college. In 1934, the Detroit "Tigers" of the American Baseball League began using the athletic field in Adair Park for spring training grounds. The Lakeland Municipal Airport was formally opened in 1934. During World War II 4,000 Army personnel occupied Drane Field in Lakeland to train bomber crews for B-26 bombers, before the men were shipped overseas to put their training in practice.

Greetings from Lakeland. **L-Fishing here is great; A-Lake Morton Drive; K-Munn Park; E-Mirror Lake Bandstand; L-Lake Hollingsworth; A-Civic Center; N-Civic Center; D-Civic Center. Circa 1930s, $3-5.**

Lake Morton Drive in Lakeland. Advertising postcard for "The Floridian" and "The Seminole" trains of the Illinois Central Railroad System. Circa 1920s, $1-3.

Lakeland. Civic Center on Mirror Lake. Cancelled 1948, $1-3.

Lakeland. Main Street in Lakeland. Circa 1920s, $4-6.

Lakeland. Main Street looking east in Lakeland. Cancelled 1949, $1-3.

Oldsmar

A short drive northwest from Tampa, along the bay, sits the town of Oldsmar. The inventor of the Oldsmobile, Ransom Eli Olds, purchased the land in 1913. He patterned the city after Washington, D.C. Olds had big plans for his city, including farms, casinos and golf courses. Some of his ideas came to fruition while others did not. In 1925, to gain identification value during the Florida land boom, the name was changed to Tampa Shores, but the old name was restored in 1937.

Tampa Downs, a thoroughbred horse race track, is centrally located in the Tampa Bay area in Oldsmar. The track had its inaugural race in 1926. The racetrack underwent restoration in 1932. During World War II the U.S. Army built barracks and turned the track into a jungle warfare-training center. In 1947 the track opened as Sunshine Park. In 1966 it was renamed Florida Downs and Turf Club, and in 1980, the new name was Tampa Bay Downs.

Tampa Bay Downs. **Tampa Bay Downs, located in Oldsmar, is the only thoroughbred horse racing track in central Florida. Former names of the track, which started operating in 1926, were Tampa Downs, Sunshine Park, and Florida Downs and Turf Club. Circa 1980, $1-3.**

Oldsmar Bay Bridge. **Oldsmar had its beginning in 1917, when Ransom E. Olds, pioneer automobile manufacturer from Lansing, Michigan, came into possession of 37,500 acres of land situated on Old Tampa Bay, partly in Hillsborough and partly in Pinellas counties. Shown is the bridge across Old Tampa Bay between Oldsmar and Safety Harbor. Cancelled 1925, $2-4.**

Plant City

Plant City, located east of Tampa, is named not for the strawberry plant for which it is now famous, but for Henry B. Plant, Florida's west coast railway pioneer. In 1839 the area was designated on a map as Fort Fraser. The town was established in 1846 at the site of the Indian village, Itchepackessa. In 1883 when Henry Plant's railroad passed through this area, land developer J.T. Evers named the town Plant City; two years later the town was incorporated. While Plant City is famed as the winter strawberry capital of the world, it is home to a lesser-known attraction of global proportions—the world's largest dinosaur exhibit, Dinosaur World, an outdoor museum of prehistoric life.

Plant City. **West Reynolds Street in Plant City. Circa 1920s, $12-14.**

Downtown Plant City. **Cancelled 1967, $1-3.**

Plant City High School. **Circa 1940s, $3-5.**

Ruskin

Around 1910, George M. Miller, president of Ruskin College in Illinois, sought a more temperate climate and moved the college to this site. The town was named for the college, which in turn was named for English author and critic John Ruskin. The soil here is especially adapted to growing tomatoes because the muck land, under-laid with marl, permits irrigation without loss of fertilizer. Numerous artesian wells provide ample water supply. Ruskin is located near Tampa Bay, south of Tampa.

Safety Harbor

Safety Harbor, located at the north end of Tampa Bay, is home to five natural springs. In 1539, when Spanish explorer Hernando De Soto made landfall in the area, he called them Springs of the Holy Spirit. Native Americans bathed in their waters for centuries. Narvaez marched into the territory after his landing at Boca Ciega Bay in 1529.

The first known white man to take up residence in the vicinity was French doctor Odet Philippe. Here, in 1823, the doctor and his slaves cleared the land and established a new plantation. In 1839 he established a fishery to supply the garrison at Fort Brooke in Tampa. In 1848 a hurricane swept away Philippe's home and slave quarters, and damaged his citrus groves. Philippe died in 1869.

Many Indian mounds at Safety Harbor were excavated by the Smithsonian Institution in 1930; the principal one is a large mound with a flat top and precipitous sides; fifty yards west is a small shell mound, seven feet high; and beyond it, is a low circular mound, forty feet in diameter. The mounds contain both pre- and post-Columbian objects; shell and bone artifacts have been found deep in the mounds.

First known as Espiritu Santo, "holy spirit," later it was called Green Springs, and finally it was incorporated as Safety Harbor in 1917. The springs earned the city its reputation as a health resort in the early 1900s. The water even was bottled and sent around the world, promising to bestow good health. The Safety Harbor Museum portrays the story of the springs throughout history.

***Ruskin*. Ruskin, just south of Tampa, is called the "Salad Bowl" because of the large number of vegetables grown there. The main crop is tomatoes. Shown is the Ruskin Woman's Club House. Circa 1920s, $3-5.**

***Safety Harbor*.**
A small, rural town in Northeast Pinellas County, it was first settled by Dr. Odet Phillippi in 1823. Early names of the town were Espiritu Santo, Green Springs, and in 1917, it was incorporated as Safety Harbor, which indicates that it is a shelter for seamen and vessels. Shown is the St. James Hotel in Safety Harbor. Circa 1920s, $5-7.

***Safety Harbor*. Safety Harbor is famed as "The Health-Giving City," a city "Where Healing Waters Flow." Most of the activities centered around mineral baths. Shown is Pipkins Mineral Wells Hotel that overlooks Tampa Bay. Circa 1920s, $4-6.**

St. Leo

In 1886, four Benedictine monks from Germany were sent from Belmont Abbey in North Carolina to minister to the spiritual needs of Seminole Indians and German-Americans in the area. The monastery and subsequent college community, located northeast of Tampa, were named for St. Leo or Leo the Great, who was Pope Leo I, 440-461. The St. Leo Abbey was one of the first Benedictine missions established in Florida.

***St. Leo*. St. Edward Hall, St. Leo College Preparatory School in St. Leo. Circa 1930s, $1-3.**

Tarpon Springs

Tarpon Springs is located on the Gulf of Mexico, northwest of Tampa. Native-born Americans had started the Florida sponge industry in this area, plucking the sponges from the sea bottom with long hooked poles. In 1905 a handful of Greek islanders came to this area with their diving suits. The new technique was more than four times as efficient as the old method, and the Greeks took over the industry. For over 100 years Tarpon Springs has been a sponge town; the Sponge Exchange, the only one in the country, is now on the National Register of Historical Sites. The Greeks brought with them their speech, their religion, and a whole colorful Mediterranean way of life. Tarpon Springs also attracted northern businessmen who saw its climate and scenic beauty as a sound investment. They turned Tarpon Springs into a charming winter resort for affluent families as well as a year-round home for themselves.

***Greetings from Tarpon Springs*. The sponge industry, which once flourished off Key West, moved to Tarpon Springs during the Spanish-American War of 1898 because of the sponger's fear of Spanish warships. Circa 1930s, $3-5.**

***Tarpon Springs*. Looking east on busy Tarpon Avenue. Tarpon Springs is on the Anclote River and the Gulf of Mexico just north of Tampa. One of the largest sponge markets, Tarpon Springs was incorporated as a city in 1887. The city owes much of its success to Greek immigrants who began to arrive in the early 1900s. The town is now extremely popular with tourists. Circa 1920s, $5-7.**

Tarpon Springs. A sightseeing boat at the Tarpon Springs Sponge Exchange. Circa 1920s, $2-4.

Deep Sea Diver. Greek divers came to Tarpon Springs to expand the sponge industry. This view illustrates a diver collecting sponges. Circa 1930s, $1-3.

Sponge Diver. Greeks have been spongers as far back as recorded history. The sponge, an article of commerce since long before the Christian era, is the skeleton of an animal that adheres to the bottom of the sea, a rock, or a coral reef. Circa 1920s, $1-3.

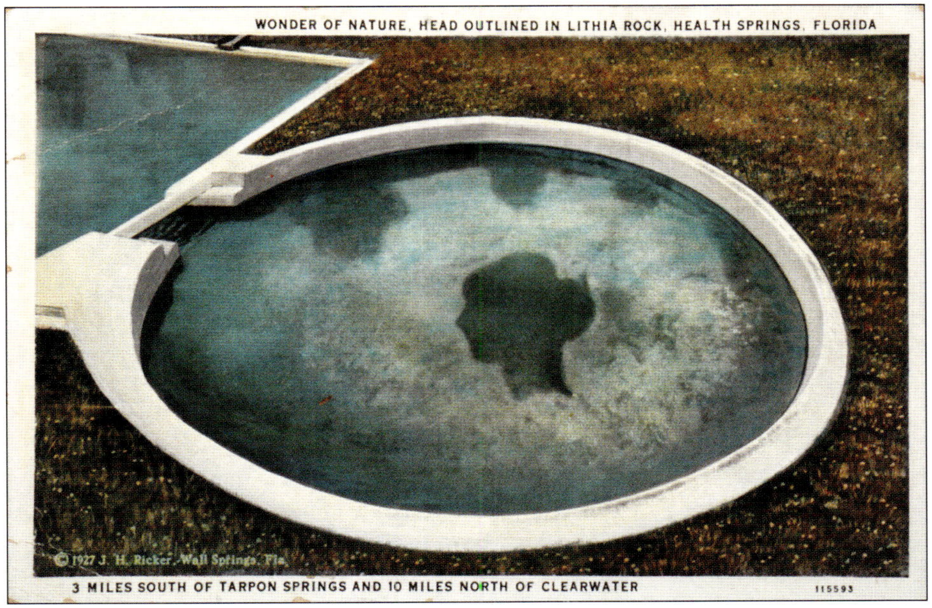

Health Springs. A wonder of nature — a head outlined in Lithia Rock at Health Springs, three miles south of Tarpon Springs. As the story goes, the outline of the head in the spring is said to be that of Ponce de Leon's wife. The head is a natural formation in solid Lithia Rock. The spring flows 200,000 gallons per hour and empties into the swimming pool. Circa 1927, $1-3.

Weeki Wachee

Weeki Wachee, a city and theme park, is located at one of Florida's great natural springs on the Gulf of Mexico, north of Tampa. The city calls itself the "City of Mermaids." This is a fitting title since mermaids have been performing here and delighting audiences for more than sixty years.

In 1947, Newton Perry, an ex-Navy frogman who had purchased the land a year earlier, presented the first live underwater Mermaid Show to the public. American Broadcasting Company (ABC) took over Weeki Wachee Spring in 1959 and, for the next twenty years, expanded and improved the Mermaid program. The operation of the springs exchanged hands again, however, all owners have continued the tradition of improving the main attraction begun by Newton Perry—the Mermaid Show. Guests sit below the spring's surface and watch mermaids perform. The performers do musical numbers such as Tribute to America and The Little Mermaid. The remarkable mermaids even eat and drink underwater. Today the theater seats five hund red people and is embedded in the side of the spring, sixteen feet below the surface.

***Weeki Wachee Mermaids*. Weeki Wachee Springs, located north of Tampa, is the surfacing point of a huge underground river. The spring, measuring one hundred feet across, has been explored to depths of one hundred fifty feet and probed another four hundred feet with lights. Divers still have not located the bottom of this miraculous body of water that pumps out 170 million gallons of water every twenty-four hours. Shown are some of the mermaids who perform in the crystal clear waters of the springs. Circa 1960s, $3-5.**

***Weeki Wachee Springs Brochure*. Circa 1960, $4-6.**

Underwater Theater. Mermaids performing in the Underwater Theater at Weeki Wachee Springs. This is the world's only underwater theater where beautiful mermaids put on underwater shows. Circa 1960s, $3-5.

Mermaids at Weeki Wachee Springs. Circa 1960s, 2-4.

Winter Haven

Winter Haven, located east of Tampa, has been a destination for millions of tourists over the past sixty years because of the drawing power and enduring popularity of Cypress Gardens. There are about one hundred spring-fed lakes within five miles of the city hall. The city was founded around 1885 and named by P.D. Eyclesheimer because it was considered a haven from cold winters.

Dick Pope is the genius who first saw a beautiful garden to which millions would flock, in the wild moss-hung cypress swamp bordering and even marching out into Lake Eloise, near Winter Haven. He dreamed. Then he acted. He bought acres of swamp and native tangled jungle and then built the gardens—Cypress Gardens. In addition to the gardens, there is a Water Ski Show that features some of America's best water skiers.

***Winter Haven*. West Park Street looking south in Winter Haven. Circa 1920s, $2-4.**

***Brookville*. The First National Bank at Brooksville. Circa 1920s, $7-9.**

***Brookville*. Brookville, located a few miles east of Weeki Wachee Springs, is the largest city in the area. Shown is the Tangerine Hotel. Circa 1920s, $3-5.**

Winter Haven. A field of gardenias in Idylwyld Gardens in Winter Haven. This young lady certainly has one of the most fragrant jobs in the world. Circa 1930s, $1-3.

Cypress Gardens. Nestled among majestic Cypress trees on the bank of Lake Eloise in Winter Haven is Cypress Gardens—the state's founding father of theme parks. Since it opened in 1936, Scarlett O'Hara-like Southern Belles have meandered the grounds adding to reasons why tourists visit the attraction. In 1943, the park debuted its Water Ski Show—a yin and yang contrast of swimsuit-clad skiers, performing highly athletic water-skiing acrobatics. Circa 1940s, $1-3.

Cypress Gardens. The lofty trunks of the tall Cypress trees provide a cathedral-like corridor for the opening trail through the gardens, while the winding waterways rival those of far off lands. Circa 1960s, $1-3.

Cypress Gardens.
Beautiful aqua maids performing in the Water Ski Show. Circa 1950s, $1-3.

Water Ski Show. Shown is a crowd watching the Water Ski Show at Cypress Gardens. Circa 1950s, $2-4.

Cypress Gardens.
Adagio act as seen during the Water Ski Show. Circa 1950s, $1-3.

Zephyrhills

Civil War veteran, Captain Howard B. Jeffries created Zephyrhills, located northeast of Tampa, as a home for veterans. Formerly known as Abbott's Station, the town delighted prospective residents with its gentle hills and terrain. The city was incorporated in 1914.

Seven of Florida's deepest springs provide the water that makes the city of Zephyrhills a household name. Deep in the Florida aquifer, a geological formation called the "Pasco High" is the source of the crystal-clear water. Limestone, silt and sand naturally filter the underground water supply and imbue it with minerals. Zephyrhills is known as the "City of Pure Water.

Zephyrhills. Fifth Avenue looking east in Zephyrhills. Circa 1910, $20-22.

Chapter Fifteen:

Clearwater

David B. Turner receives credit for naming Clearwater. It was Turner who, in 1859, used the name, Clear Water Harbor, on an application for a U.S. Post Office. The town was incorporated in 1891. "Clear Water" became one word in 1895, and "Harbor" was dropped from the name in 1906. But Clearwater's history goes back many centuries. What took the white man a long time to discover, the Indians had enjoyed since ancient times. There was an abundance of fish in the waters and game in the woods, the climate was pleasant and healthful, and the scenery and surroundings were delightful. Because they left great mounds, the early people have become known as the Mound Builders. Many of the mounds were made entirely of shells, indicating they were refuse dumps of the shellfish-eating Indians. The white man, in modern times, put the contents of these mounds to use—to make shell roads.

The Beginning of a City

Clearwater got its first newspaper in 1873. The founding editor of the Clear Water Times was a minister, the Rev. C.S. Reynolds who had founded the Tampa Herald in 1854. As the decade of the 1880s began, Clearwater got its first hotel, the Orange Bluff Hotel. This hotel, along with several cottages built in connection with it, opened Clearwater as a resort of sorts, and a few tourists began to come. The most important development of the decade was the coming of the railroad to Clearwater and the Pinellas peninsula. It was the Orange Belt narrow gauge railroad that ran from Sanford to St. Petersburg. At the time, only about eighteen families lived here. There were no paved streets and no improvements.

In 1895, the only paved streets were Cleveland Street from the harbor to the small Orange Belt Railroad station, and Fort Harrison Avenue from Cleveland to a point south of the Methodist church. The streets were paved with shell removed from an old Indian mound near the harbor.

Greetings from Clearwater. **Clearwater, the county seat of Pinellas County, is located north of St. Petersburg and across the Causeway from Tampa. The town was first called Clear Water Harbor because of a spring of sulphur water bubbling up in the Gulf of Mexico near the shore, making the water unusually clear and sparkling. Later the name was changed to Clearwater. Circa 1930s, $3-5.**

Also in 1895 the Orange Belt Railroad became part of the Plant System. This was the operation of the fabulous Henry B. Plant who had brought his railroad over to Tampa and built the Tampa Bay Hotel, which opened in 1891.

Plant was recognized as one of Florida's greatest nineteenth century railroad developers and, more than any other person, was responsible for the growth of central and western Florida. Plant was also responsible for one of the most attractive landmarks in the Clearwater area—the fantastic Belleview Hotel.

Belleview Hotel

With its white walls, green gabled roofs, and spacious grounds overlooking Clearwater's scenic bay, the expansive Belleview Hotel has been a west coast landmark since 1897. Railroad magnate Henry Bradley Plant built the Belleview and gave the Florida west coast not only a rail link to the outside world, but other magnificent accommodations, including the ornate Tampa Bay Hotel in Tampa, and others on the sun coast.

The Belleview opened its doors to the wealthy vacationers who came from all parts of the world. It became popular overnight, the mecca of the railroad giants, steel magnates, utility kings, industrial barons and socialites. Bringing their famed owners to Florida sunshine, as many as fifteen private railroad cars would park on special sidings of the hotel. Famous guests: How's the Duke of Windsor for a starter. Norman Vincent Peale found it a favorite retreat. Back in the early days, the guests included the Disstons of the Philadelphia Disston tools firm, the Whelan family of Whelan Drugs, and the Ford family of the glass firm in Detroit. By 1915 the golf plant at the Belleview had been expanded to two 18-hole courses, designed by Donald J. Ross, dean of American golf architects. The Belleview attracted big names in golf including Bobby Jones, Grantland

Street Scene. **An early Clearwater street scene prior to paved streets. Note the two-wheeled cart being pulled by a white horse, an early mode of transportation. Cancelled 1909, $10-12**

Boat Docks. **Private docks in Clear Water Harbor, which was so shallow that long docks were necessary for boat traffic. The longest one was the city dock where the Madison packet brought the mail, goods, and visitors from Cedar Key prior to 1888. Circa 1905, $6-8.**

Rice, Rex Beach, Gene Sarazen, Walter Hagen, Tommy Harmon, and Babe Didrickson. The six hundred-room Belleview bade welcome to many northern visitors, many of whom made golf history on the Belleview golf courses. The Belleview (now Belleview Biltmore) Hotel is located just south of Clearwater at Belleair.

Twentieth Century Progress

In 1900 J. N. McClung built the first ice factory here; this was the beginning of a water system for the community. The Clearwater Pier Company built a public dock and pavilion at the foot of Cleveland Street in 1902. A couple of years later, these facilities were donated to the city. In 1905, Clearwater was illuminated when an electric light franchise was granted to J.N. McClung. Business leaders formed a Board of Trade in 1905, a predecessor to the Chamber of Commerce.

Clearwater's first courthouse was built in 1912. Its successor was built seven years later. In 1914 the Morton F. Plant Hospital opened. It was named in honor of Morton F. Plant, an early civic leader of Clearwater who put up the bulk of the money needed to build. The city got a public library in 1916, under a grant from Andrew Carnegie.

Early on, the town led a quiet existence. But in the 1920s, the city had its first look as speculators inflated real estate values, only to see them plunge a few years later.

The city lost a piece of its early heritage in 1927, when the modern Million Dollar Causeway, later renamed Memorial Causeway, replaced an early wooden structure known as "the Rickety Bridge."

On June 28, 1934 the Davis Causeway opened, including a 3,510-foot bridge. The roadway was twenty-four feet wide, smooth and straight, connecting Tampa and the mainland with Clearwater and the Gulf beaches. It was a toll facility that cost fifty cents for a round trip ticket, including passenger car, for all passengers. After World War II the causeway was widened and improved and renamed "Courtney Campbell Parkway" to honor Courtney W. Campbell, who lived in Clearwater.

The magnificent Belleview Hotel was leased to the U.S. Air Force in 1942 for use as an auxiliary barracks for MacDill and Drew Fields in Tampa. About 3,000 Air Force personnel were housed at one time on the premises. The practice range and part of one of the golf courses were used as drill grounds. The hotel was returned to its owners in 1944.

World War II brought another time of prosperity. Residents used the war to cash in on the influx of soldiers into the Tampa Bay area. Clearwater also contributed to the war effort in a more tangible way. A local resident, Donald Roebling, invented the Alligator, an amphibious vehicle that the Allies used to assail Pacific Islands controlled by the Japanese.

The postwar era led to the city's next great boom. Between 1950 and 1957, Clearwater grew at a pace unequaled by any American city. The population more than doubled, shooting up from 15,000 to 33,000. The growth inevitably strangled much of the rural areas of Clearwater, and many landowners began to sell off to developers. The result is a city of 100,000 people in 1990.

Clearwater Episcopal Church. **The old wooden Episcopal Church on South Fort Harrison Avenue. The church was later enlarged, but the property was sold in 1924. The Clearwater Courthouse was later built on the property. Cancelled 1910, $3 5.**

Davis Causeway. **In 1934, Davis Causeway, 9.5 miles long, across beautiful Old Tampa Bay, connected Tampa with Clearwater and the Gulf beaches. After World War II the causeway was widened and improved and renamed Courtney Campbell Parkway to honor Courtney W Campbell, who lived in Clearwater. Circa 1930s, $1-3.**

Cleveland Street. **South side of Cleveland Street looking east. Cars parked diagonally on both sides of the street in downtown Clearwater. Circa 1920s, $4-6.**

Clearwater Bank. The Bank of Clearwater at Cleveland Street and Fort Harrison Avenue long dominated the downtown scene. The bank was the city's oldest and largest and was organized in 1906 with $18,000 capital stock. Circa 1920s, $3-5.

Street Scene. This is Ft. Harrison Avenue looking North from Cleveland Street. Cancelled 1923, $3-5.

Playing in the Sand. This view shows sunbathers enjoying the sand at Clearwater Beach. Note the bathing caps the ladies are wearing. Circa 1920s, $6-8.

Public Dock and Pavilion. This view shows the two-story pavilion at the foot of Cleveland Street. This recreational facility, built in 1902, included a park that overlooked Tampa Bay. The street was unpaved. The pavilion was used for dances on the second floor and a fish house on the bottom floor. The pier was used as a steamboat stop. Circa 1908, $6-8.

Belleview Hotel. With its white walls, green gabled roofs, and spacious grounds overlooking Clearwater's scenic bay, the expansive Belleview Hotel (later Belleview Biltmore Hotel) has been a west coast landmark since 1896. The hotel has more than two miles of corridors and requires 1,000 gallons of paint for one exterior coat. This view was taken from the golf course. Cancelled 1911, $6-8.

Belleair.
The road to the beach at Belleair. The name of this area was given by Henry B. Plant in 1896, when he purchased most of the land now included in the town and built his Belleview Hotel. Belleair Beach, once a desolate sand spur thick with Norfolk pines, is now filled with high-rise buildings. Circa 1908, $2-4.

Clearwater Beach. Winter, Summer, Spring or Fall — any time is the best time of all. Playing is any time on Clearwater Beach on the Gulf of Mexico. Clearwater Beach is connected with the mainland by a landscaped two-mile causeway. The broad, white beach attracts both residents and visitors. Who wouldn't like a relaxing, fun-filled day at Clearwater Beach? Circa 1920s, $4-6.

Bathing in the Gulf.
Sun worshippers regularly fill the public beaches on the Gulf of Mexico. Shown are bathers enjoying the beach and water at Clearwater Beach. The cooling waters of the Gulf of Mexico refreshed bathers, while fishing and sailing entertained other folks. Cancelled 1926, $6-8.

Clearwater Beach Pavilion.
The new Pavilion at Clearwater Beach attracted huge crowds in the 1920s. It was razed in the 1930s. Circa 1920s, $2-4

Clearwater City Hall. The Clearwater City Hall was an attractive brick structure. Circa 1930s, $3-5.

Mid-century Clearwater Beach. Popular Clearwater Beach in the late 1940s. Men were wearing topless suits by then, and the ladies were daring in their two-piece suits. Circa 1949, $1-3.

Gray Moss Inn.
The elegant Gray Moss Inn on South Fort Harrison Avenue. Fords were the popular vehicle in the Roaring Twenties, as evidenced here. Cancelled 1933, $2-4.

Another Beach Scene. Sunning, picture-taking, or building sand castles were pastimes occupied by visitors on popular Clearwater Beach. Cancelled 1948, $1-3.

Causeway. A 1940s view of the Courtney Campbell Parkway that links Tampa with Clearwater and the Gulf of Mexico beaches. Cancelled 1950, $1-3.

Kapok Tree.
This Kapok Tree Inn postcard shows the Kapok Tree that was brought from India as a seedling over 150 years ago. Circa 1960, $1-3.

Chapter Sixteen:

St. Petersburg

One of the city's most famous landmarks, the Million Dollar Pier, opened in 1926. Popular dances were held at the pier. Shops, card parties, sing-alongs, and live radio shows attracted not only tourists but also residents. In spring each year, high school students decorated the ballroom for their senior class proms. In 1973 the recreational palace was replaced with a modern inverted pyramid structure. This upended pyramid became St. Petersburg's top-selling scenic postcard.

In 1928, Thomas Rowe from Norfolk, Virginia built the luxury-filled, ten-story, 220-room Don CeSar Beach Resort & Spa on St. Petersburg Beach. The rouge-colored (often called the "Pink Palace") beach front resort took its name from Don Caesar, the leading character in Rowe's favorite opera, *Maritana*. The final cost for the Don CeSar was more than $1.2 million, three hundred percent more than the original budget. The hotel had modern porcelain bathtubs, verandas, and 13,900 windows that bathed guests in the Florida sun. Each room featured a mahogany writing desk, a horsehair mattress and an original rug. Famous guests poured into the hotel including author F. Scott Fitzgerald, gangster Al Capone, attorney Clarence Darrow, and Lou Gehrig and the Yankee baseball team. The U.S. Army purchased the Don CeSar for use during World War II. It became a convalescent center for battle-weary airmen, offering them a place to regain their physical and mental strength. After the war, the hotel became a Veterans' Administration regional office building. Several years – and several renovations – later, the resort reclaimed its title as the "Pink Palace." It remains on the National Register of Historic Places.

A small flying field along the waterfront south of Central Avenue in 1929 was named Whitted Field after the St. Petersburg aviator Albert Whitted, who served as a flying instructor during World War I; he was killed in a plane crash near Pensacola in 1923. The field also housed a hangar for Goodyear blimps that began flying out of St. Petersburg in 1929. Whitted Field also was the birthplace of National Airlines (1934), which later became part of Pan American Airlines.

Though St. Petersburg's population nearly tripled during the decade, from 14,237 in 1920 to 40,425 in 1930, having more people put a strain on the citizens already living there. Jobs became scarce, and so did money. Fortunately, everyone was unaware of a greater financial bust about to confront them: "Black Thursday" — the day of the Stock Market crash in October 1929, which turned much of America topsy-turvy. St. Petersburg already was saturated with bad news in its own marketplace, so the Wall Street failure appeared more of a sequel than an interruption to its economy.

As expected, prices everywhere hit rock bottom. But none reached the low level advertised by Doc Webb's Drug Store. Webb made national news with an astonishing three-cent breakfast. It included a glass of orange juice, an egg, a strip of bacon, a piece of toast, and a cup of coffee. Needless to say, thousands ate breakfast together every morning at the Webb City counter. Everybody, it seemed, could come up with three cents. Many citizens, however, lost their homes because they could not pay their taxes.

The Florida Military Academy purchased the closed Rolyat Hotel in 1932 and opened a military prep school for grades one through twelve. The school closed twenty years later and now houses the Stetson Law School.

A significant day in aviation occurred on October 1, 1934, when a four-passenger plane took off from Whitted Field in St. Petersburg, headed for Daytona Beach.

Florida's oldest botanical gardens opened in 1935 as a public attraction. When founded in 1903 by George Turner, Sr., the Sunken Gardens were not much more than a sinkhole and a muddy, shallow lake. Turner turned the six-acre area into a garden with winding paths, stream-spanning bridges, quiet lagoons, cascading waterfalls, and thousands of tropical plants and trees. Exotic birds and other wildlife are found in the enclosures along the garden trails.

The economy, residential population and the number of winter visitors declined through the 1930s. St. Petersburg dragged itself into 1940, but again the population

Wish You Were Here. Bathing beauties posing for a "Welcome to St. Petersburg message." Circa 1930s, $10-12.

had increased over the decade, from 40,425 to 60,812. It was the smallest gain, percentage-wise, since the city's founding.

World War II breathed life into a St. Petersburg that had suffered following the land bust of the 1920s, the depression, and a declining tourist industry. After the Japanese attack on Pearl Harbor and the declaration of war by the United States, thousands of U.S. military personnel invaded the Tampa Bay area. Overnight, almost every hotel and apartment building in St. Petersburg was put to use by the military as barracks. Pass-A-Grill, a small community south of St. Petersburg, was used as a site for anti-aircraft gun emplacements. This called for building a watchtower, barracks, theater, Post Exchange, and many administrative and storage buildings. Many men from the base spent leisure time in nearby St. Petersburg. Today, residents can remember seeing military personnel on Central Avenue, lining up for meals in hotels that had been converted to barracks and mess halls. Following World War II, St. Petersburg again became a popular resort center and the number of visitors steadily increased. Many later chose to retire to the city.

Still a baseball town, the city now boasted Spring Training sites for two Major League teams. For the comfort of the thousands of tourists coming down for the March and April games, in 1947 the city built Al Lang Field on the waterfront.

The Skyway Bridge, connecting St. Petersburg with Bradenton, Sarasota and points south, opened in 1954. The 864-foot main span steel structure stretched a little over four miles in length. The fanfare surrounding the opening of the bridge included ten bathing suit clad beauties, each representing a different Gulf Coast community. They were on hand to assist Governor Charley Johns as he officially opened the $22 million bridge. The Skyway played host to over 15,000 cars that day, which had lined up to be among the first to cross the bridge. From that day on, Pinellas and Manatee counties, before over an hour apart, were now separated by a quick ten-minute drive. In 1971, a second span was added to the bridge, and in 1987, a new ultra-modern, $245 million Skyway Bridge replaced the former structure.

The city's new stability and metropolitan attracted academia-minded institutions — in 1954, Stetson University College of Law took over the closed Rolyat Hotel, and nine years later, Eckerd College opened a campus off 34th Street South.

The historic downtown of St. Petersburg was placed on the National Register of Historic Places. It is bounded by Fifth Avenue North on the north, Central Avenue on the south, Dr. M.L. King (9th) Street North on the west, and Tampa Bay on the east. It contains more than four hundred buildings, eighty percent of which are considered historic.

***St. Petersburg*. The largest city in Pinellas County and a popular retirement and resort city. The Sunshine City was named after one of the coldest great cities in the world, Russia's St. Petersburg. John C. Williams of Detroit, St. Petersburg's founder, acquired acreage in 1876, which became the nucleus of the city. In the 1920s so sure of daily sunshine were the residents of St. Petersburg that one of the city's publishers gave away the entire home edition of their paper every day that the sun failed to make an appearance before it went to press. 1927 was the first year that Mayor Lew Brown did not have to give away a free copy of his paper. Circa 1930s, $3-5.**

Central Avenue.
An 1897 view of Central Avenue taken from the top of the smokestack of the old electric light plant at the foot of Central Avenue. The Detroit Hotel can be seen on the right. Cancelled 1909, $8-10.

Music in the Park.
This view shows people attending a band concert at the Pavilion in St. Petersburg's City Park (later it became Williams Park). The Pavilion, built in 1895, was a popular gathering place in the early 1900s. In 1920 the Pavilion was replaced with a bandstand in the shape of a half-shell. Circa 1908, $2-4.

A Walk in the Park. In 1900 many of the streets in St. Petersburg were not paved. Long-skirted women often complained of mud streets and no sidewalks. This postcard view shows a lady and two girls walking in Williams Park. Cancelled 1911, $3-5.

Detroit Hotel. Built in 1888, about the time the railroad reached St. Petersburg, the 100-room Detroit Hotel was one of only two buildings which could be seen from the railroad depot. The Detroit Hotel, the first in St. Petersburg, was a fine hotel for a town with less than fifty inhabitants. The hotel was so far ahead of its time for years that it loomed in majestic splendor on a lot facing a sand street. Circa 1908, $6-8.

Huntington Hotel.
A view of the Huntington Hotel that was built in the 1890s. Circa 1910, $5-7.

View Along the Shore.
This postcard, mailed in 1910, shows the waterfront in downtown St. Petersburg. This is how the waterfront looked before it was developed by the city. Cancelled 1910, $2-4.

Pier Fishing. Fishing for sheephead, mackerel and shark from the Atlantic Coast Line railroad pier. The pier was also a popular recreational spot. Circa 1910, $6-8.

Indian Shell Mound. A view of a large sand and shell Tocobaga Indian Mound in St. Petersburg. The only record of the earliest inhabitants of the St. Petersburg area are the shell mounds and the comparatively few implements they contain. These mounds were the dwelling places of the earliest inhabitants of the region and contained trash consisting of discarded shells of shellfish gathered for food.

The prehistoric Indian Mound shown was about thirty feet tall and was located on the present grounds of Bayfront Medical Center. In the 1920s, shell from this mound was used to make streets in St. Petersburg. Circa 1910, $6-8.

Fountain of Youth.
One of the city's pioneers, Edwin Tomlinson, gave St. Petersburg the Fountain of Youth, which became a nineteenth century landmark for the city. For decades, tourists and residents filled their drinking jugs with the sulphur water from this artesian well that was said to have medicinal value. Circa 1910, $6-8.

Boating on Tampa Bay. Peaceful, unharried, and magnificent are the beaches and waterways around St. Petersburg. Gulf of Mexico waters are warm, limpid and placid. Boating on the Gulf and on Tampa Bay was among the state's leading recreations. Circa 1910, $4-6.

Pass-A-Grille. At the southern tip of Long Key is one of the oldest and most interesting of the west coast beach communities. Pass-A-Grille, incorporated in 1911, was so named because fishermen stopped here to cook and grill their meals. As early as 1841, it was called Pass-aux-gril-larade on a government survey, meaning "Pass of the Grillers." This postcard shows passengers getting off a steamer at this popular St. Petersburg Beach area. Circa 1911, $12-14.

Waterfront Scene. This view shows the east end of Central Avenue as it appeared in the early 1900s. Also shown is the Atlantic Coast Line Pier. Cancelled 1911, $5-6.

Citrus Packing Plant. The Milne-O'Berry Packing Plant, established in 1919, boxed citrus fruit that was then shipped throughout the United States. Cancelled 1936, $3-5.

Picking Oranges. Shown are orange pickers at Eaton's Grove, west of Ninth Street North near Twenty-first Avenue North. This was a typical scene in St. Petersburg's orange groves.

The pickers climbed tall ladders to clean the upper limbs of the trees. The oranges were collected in field crates and moved by small trucks to nearby packing houses for shipping to markets. Circa 1914, $3-5.

St. Petersburg-Tampa Airboat Line.
The world's first commercial airline was established in St. Petersburg on January 1, 1914 when Anthony "Tony" Jannus began flying the Benoist seaplane for regularly scheduled flights between St. Petersburg and Tampa. He carried both passengers and mail. The ex-mayor of St. Petersburg paid four hundred dollars for the honor of being the first passenger. Reproduction postcard. Circa 1950, $2-4.

Port of St. Petersburg.
When the railroads clamped down on embargo during the Florida boom, Bayboro Harbor was a place of feverish activity. More than a score of ships were anchored in the harbor at one time. Circa 1915, $7-9.

Catching an Alligator.
A 1908 alligator hunt resulted in Bird Latham, manager of the St. Petersburg Electric Light and Power Company (the man holding the rope around the alligator's snout), and associates bringing home this captured reptile. Cancelled 1916, $10-12.

Advertising Postcard. This view of the four-story Florida Bank & Trust Company was mailed to prospective clients as an advertising card. In 1917 the Florida Bank ran into financial difficulties, and in 1920, it became part of the First National Bank of St. Petersburg. Cancelled 1914, $5-7.

Central National Bank.
Shown is the Central National Bank of St. Petersburg on the southwest corner of Central Avenue and Second Street as it appeared from 1912 to 1922. In 1922 the bank added a two-floor addition and changed its name to the Central National Bank and Trust Co. of St. Petersburg. Cancelled 1919, $3-5.

Open Air Post Office. The 1917 Open Air Post Office at 400 First Avenue North was the first of its kind in the world. Local architect George Stewart designed it so that people could access their post office boxes around the clock. Located in the center of the business district, the post office distributed daily a volume of mail to the thousands of visitors who crowded the outdoor loggia. Circa 1920s, $2-4.

Rolyat Hotel. In 1926, the beautiful Spanish-style Rolyat Hotel had its celebrated opening. Babe Ruth and Walter Hagen were there. The tiles that cover the structure were brought from Spain, where they were taken from the crumbling ruins of a former Iberian nobleman's home. Today the building houses the Stetson University Law School. Circa 1928, $4-6.

Don CeSar Hotel. Thomas J. Rowe built the 312-room Don CeSar Hotel in 1927. It housed troops during World War II and then served as offices of the Veterans Administration for two decades. It is now a hotel again after it had been vacant for sometime and was refurbished. Circa 1930s, $5-7.

Vinoy Park Hotel.
The Vinoy Park Hotel was one of the earliest and largest of St. Petersburg's resort hotels of the Florida "boom." The owner and promoter of the hotel was Aymer Laughner, a Pennsylvania millionaire who moved to St. Petersburg in 1920 to carry out his land development plans. The hotel opened with a gala New Year's Eve Party on December 31, 1925. The hotel is still operating today. Circa 1920s, $4-6.

Early Downtown View.
A view of downtown St. Petersburg, showing Central Avenue from Third Street. St. Petersburg has long been known as the tourist capital of Florida's West Coast. The city has over thirty-three miles of waterfront. Circa 1914, $10-12.

Traffic Jams.
A 1915 view looking southeast at the intersection of Central Avenue and Fifth Street with the La Plaza Theater on the right, the four-story Florida Bank and Trust Company building to its left, and next to the bank is the Poinsettia Hotel. Also shown are tandem streetcars, automobiles, and horse and buggy.
Circa 1914, $4-6.

Trolley System.
Philadelphian F.A. Davis started the St. Petersburg streetcar system in 1905 that was eventually purchased by the city. In 1936 the streetcars were being retired in favor of buses; the last streetcar run was in 1949. Circa 1920s, $3-5.

Central Avenue.
St. Petersburg was becoming a bustling metropolis, and Central Avenue began to have the first sign that a traffic problem was in the making. This view, taken on a busy Saturday, was between Fourth and Third streets. Cancelled 1923, $5-7.

Midwinter Crowd on Central Avenue.
The sender of this postcard, mailed in 1923, wrote, "Here is an idea of the way we dress and live on the street in St. Petersburg. The walks on Central Avenue are lined with green benches where we sit and visit with anyone who comes along." This view shows the Ansonia Hotel at the northeast corner of Fourth Street, which housed one of the early St. Petersburg post offices. Cancelled 1923, $5-7.

Street Scene.
This view shows the corner of Fourth Street and Central Avenue. The American Bank and Trust Company, one of four banks in 1917, can be seen with its white columns at 342 Central Avenue. Circa 1920s, $3-5.

Busy Corner.
An early view of a popular and busy intersection in St. Petersburg, the crossing of Central Avenue and Fifth Street. Later, the Kress Building was constructed at this location. The tall building in the rear is the Princess Martha Hotel, which opened in 1924 on First Avenue North. Circa 1926, $5-7.

First Avenue North.
This view shows First Avenue North as it looks across Williams Park. The Princess Martha Hotel is shown in the foreground and the Suwannee Hotel a block away. Period transportation is also shown in this scene — Model A automobiles and streetcar. Circa 1920s, $4-6.

Sit and Watch the World Go By.
As birds annually return to familiar old nesting places, so do these perennial winter visitors flock back to the green benches on St. Petersburg's streets, each to his or her favorite seat, to exchange views on life with other visitors. The green benches, introduced in 1907, were most popular between the 1920s and 1970s. Circa 1920s, $3-5.

Automobile Travel. The biggest event of 1924 was the opening of the Gandy Bridge toll facility between Tampa and St. Petersburg. The government bought the toll bridge from George S. Gandy in 1944 and dropped the toll charges. Circa 1920s, $2-4.

St. Petersburg Yacht Club.
The Yacht Club was organized in 1909. During 1916-17, a clubhouse was built on Bayshore Drive between First Avenue North and Central Avenue. During 1921 and 1922, an addition was added to the clubhouse. The formal opening was on December 21, 1922. Circa 1920s, $3-5.

Coliseum.
When one hears the word "Coliseum," the world-famous structure in ancient Rome usually comes to mind. However, people familiar with St. Petersburg think of a structure just north of Mirror Lake in downtown St. Petersburg. Since the grand opening in 1924, many of America's greatest performers have appeared on stage at the Coliseum. Nobody has played "Taps" for this wonderful entertainment center yet. Cancelled 1926, $8-10.

The Municipal Pier. The Million Dollar Pier was built in 1926 at the foot of Second Avenue North. The pier, which jutted a half mile into Tampa Bay, contained a two-story casino with ballroom, a restaurant, the studios of radio station WSUN, boat landings, and fishing balconies. Streetcars traveled to the end of the pier by actually going inside the first floor of the building. Driving to the end of the pier was a popular pastime in the 1920s. This view shows a Coast Guard vessel moored alongside the pier. The Coast Guard base at Bayboro Harbor opened in 1927. The Million Dollar Pier building shown was demolished in 1967. A new building with an inverted pyramid design opened in 1972. Circa 1930s, $3-5.

Florida Pelicans.
Feeding the pelicans, sea gulls, and ducks on St. Petersburg's Municipal R ecreation Pier was a popular diversion for tourists. Circa 1930s, $1-3.

Shuffleboard Courts and Coliseum. Playing shuffleboard was a favorite pastime in St. Petersburg. This view shows the courts in Mirror Lake Park, headquarters of the St. Petersburg Shuffle Board Club, which was the largest of its kind in the world. The Coliseum is shown in the background. Circa 1930s, $2-4.

A Children's Playground. Sun, sand, surf—an unbeatable combination for Florida's children. Shown are children playing at one of the St. Petersburg area playgrounds. Two of the bathers seem to be looking for shells. Circa 1915, $2-4.

The Beaches. Across the causeway from St. Petersburg is the gateway to the beaches — St. Petersburg Beach, south to Pass-A-Grille, north toward Treasure Island and Madeira Beach. Pass-A-Grille Beach had its idyllic spots in the early 1920s, as shown in this tranquil postcard scene. In bathing "costume" or not, one could enjoy the cooling breezes, the shimmering sand, or splash in the surf. Circa 1920s, $2-4.

On the Beach. Young people of the 1920s went to the beach for a day of fun and relaxation. This happy scene was at Pass-A-Grille beach. "Where will they stop?" asked many of the older generation when the young ladies took to the beach in suits baring their knees. Today the brevity of the swim suit is limited only by the young lady's modesty. Circa 1920s, $3-5.

Gulf Beaches. Beaches that make up the St. Petersburg area include Indian Rocks Beach, Redington Beach, Madeira Beach, Treasure Island, St. Petersburg Beach, and Pass-A-Grille. These beaches are knotted together in a continuous surf-splashed sandy shore that presents countless scenes of striking beauty. This hand-colored postcard was created and published by E. G. Barnhill, who produced many beautiful St. Petersburg postcards from 1914 to 1932. Circa 1930, $6-8.

Please Don't Mr. Cop! The warm sun and sand of the beach finds everyone participating in healthful recreation and fun. It is a family affair, going to the beach at St. Petersburg Beach. However, these two young beach-goers seem to be getting a bathing suit ticket for pushing the comfort limit. Circa 1930s, $4-6.

Tarpon and Pretty Lady. A prize catch being displayed by a happy angler. Outsmarting the "silver king" is a real sport indulged in by both sexes in the Gulf of Mexico waters near St. Petersburg. Around six hundred varieties of game fish, most of them edible, may be caught from the bridge, pier, small boat, or deep-sea fishing boats in and around St. Petersburg. Circa 1930s, $4-6.

Bathing Beauties. Postcards of pretty girls at the beach were as popular in the 1930s and 1940s as they are now. Bathing was an all year sport in the "Sunshine City." The Vinoy Park Hotel can be seen in the background. Circa 1940s, $2 4.

Gulfport Casino. Gulfport, adjoining St. Petersburg on the southwest, offers many attractions to its visitors. The community started in 1885 as Bonafacio, then Disston City in 1889, then Veteran City in 1906, and finally Gulfport in 1910. This postcard shows the Art Deco-style casino on Boca Ciega Bay, where dances and entertainment were enjoyed, and a large pier, extending out into the bay, and a popular bathing beach. Circa 1930s, $3-5.

They're Off! At the St. Petersburg Kennel Club.
"Going to the dogs" has a different meaning in St. Petersburg where sleek, lean and famously fast greyhounds chase the mechanical rabbit around the track in almost unbelievable bursts of speed. The St. Petersburg Kennel Club is one of the oldest dog tracks in the United States. The kennel club opened in 1925 on Gandy Boulevard a year after the completion of Gandy Bridge. It is still operating as Derby Lane. Circa 1930s, $2-4.

Peacock Farm. This postcard shows the Peacock Farm in St. Petersburg that was reputed to have had the largest collection of all the different kinds of peacocks in the United States. The multicolored strutting birds and the tropical background present a picture that, for sheer beauty, is unforgettable. Admission to the farm was thirty cents. Circa 1930s, $2-4.

Aerial View of St. Petersburg. Tropical skies, waving palms, and the limpid waters of Mirror Lake make this one of St. Petersburg's outstanding beauty spots. This is how downtown St. Petersburg looked from 3,000 feet in the air in the mid-1900s. Circa 1940, $2-4.

Webb's City. The sender of this postcard wrote "Webb City is a small city inside of St. Petersburg. Stores are open each evening until 11 o'clock. Very convenient for all visitors that come down. We go there every Saturday night. Very interesting." Lighting up the sky in the 1940s for blocks around Ninth Street South were the many stores in the Webb's City mercantile complex. Many nights, towering, spinning Ferris wheels and carnival rides brought in by "Doc" Webb also lit up the horizon, beckoning shoppers from miles around. Cancelled 1949, $2-4.

Sunshine Skyway.
The Sunshine Skyway, connecting St. Petersburg with Bradenton and Sarasota, was one of the most spectacular bridges in America. The bridge covers eleven miles of open water where Tampa Bay meets the Gulf of Mexico. The Sunshine Skyway opened in 1954, followed by construction of a second span in 1971. In 1987 a new ultra-modern bridge replaced the former structures. Circa 1950s, $1-3.

About the Postcard

Postcards had their beginning in Austria in 1869. The United States government began to issue postcards in 1873. The cards were stamped on one side to provide for the address and left blank on the other side. The picture postcard did not come into common use in the United States until after 1900. It was about 1902 that the postcard craze hit the country, lasting up to our entry into World War I in the spring of 1917. Collectors would send postcards to total strangers in faraway places, asking local cards in return. Some collectors specialized in railroad depots, street scenes, cemeteries, churches, courthouses, farms, amusement parks, rivers, steamboats, plants, agricultural products, even comic cards; others collected anything they could find. Postcard albums, bought by the millions, were filled with every sort of postcard ever issued. The craze was actually worldwide, since many countries had postcards.

Before March 1, 1907, it was illegal to write any message on the same side of the card as the address. For that reason the early postcards often have handwriting all over the sides of the picture, and sometimes right across it. Many an otherwise beautiful card was defaced in this way. When postcards first started to go through the mails, they were postmarked at the receiving post office as well as that of the sender, making it easy to see the time involved between post offices—sometimes remarkably brief! The volume of postcards was an important reason for discontinuing the unnecessary second marking about 1910. For years postcards cost only a nickel for six and the postage was a penny, right up to World War II.

The most popular American postcards up to World War I were those made in Germany from photographs supplied by American publishers. At the time of the postcard craze, of course, color photography was still something of a rarity and not commercially viable. For the color cards, black and white photos were touched up, hand-colored, and then generally reproduced by lithography. Lithography consists of transferring the image to a lithographic stone, offset to a rubber blanket, and then printed onto paper. The details in the German produced cards were extremely sharp, and the best of them technically have never been matched since.

The German postcard industry folded in the summer of 1914, when the war struck Europe, and never revived. Three years later, the United States entered the war, and the postcard craze ended.

Postcards printed in America were generally of a poorer quality and had a white border. These white border cards were produced until about 1930 when the "linen" textured card was introduced. While this card was less expensive to produce, it also reduced the clarity of detail in the pictures. After 1945 the "chrome" card with a glossy finish replaced the linen card. This type of finish allowed for a very sharp reproduction of the picture. In 1970, a king-sized chrome card (4 by 5.875 inches) was introduced and by 1978 it was in general use everywhere.

Bibliography

A History of Tampa Bay Hotel. Tampa, Florida: University of Tampa Foundation.

Arsenault, Raymond. *St. Petersburg And The Florida Dream, 1888-1950*. Gainesville, Florida: University Press of Florida, 1996.

Ayers, R. Wayne. *Florive Tampa Bay*. Manteo, North Carolina: The Insiders' Guides Inc., 1996.

Dunn, Hampton. *Tampa: A Pictorial History*. Norfolk, Virginia: Donning Company Publishers, 1985.

Yesterday's Clearwater. Miami, Florida: E.A. Seemann Publishing, 1974.

Yesterday's Tampa. Miami, Florida: E. A. Seemann Publishing, Inc., 1972.

Dunn, Hampton, Editor. *The Sunland Tribune, Vol. III, No. 1*. Tampa, Florida: Tampa Historical Society, 1977.

The Sunland Tribune, Vol. VII, No. 1. Tampa, Florida: Tampa Historical Society, 1981.

Fuller, Walter. *St. Petersburg and Its People*. St. Petersburg, Florida: Great Outdoors Publishing Company, 1972.

Frisbie, Louise K. *Florida's Fabled Inns*. Bartow, Florida: Imperial Publishing Company, 1980.

Grismer, Karl H. *Tampa*. St. Petersburg, Florida: St. Petersburg Printing Co. 1950.

Harner, Charles E. *A Pictorial History of Ybor City*. Tampa, Florida: Trend Publications, Inc., 1975.

Homan, Lynn M. and Thomas Reilly. *Wings Over Florida*. Charleston, South Carolina: Arcadia Publishing, 1999.

Jackson, Page S. *An Informal History of St. Petersburg*. St. Petersburg, Florida: Great Outdoors Publishing Company, 1992.

Kaiser, Robert J. *Tampa: The Early Years*. Charleston, South Carolina: Arcadia Publishing, 1999.

Kaserman, James. *Gasparilla, Pirate Genius*. Fort Myers, Florida: Pirate Publishing International, 2000.

Kleinberg, Eliot. *Historical Traveler's Guide to Florida*. Sarasota, Florida: Pineapple Press, 2006.

Lenfestey, Hatty, Editor. *Moments In Time: The Tampa Bay Hotel*. Tampa, Florida: Henry B. Plant Museum.

Marth, Del R. and Martha J. Marth. *St. Petersburg: Once Upon A Time*. Branford, Florida: Suwannee River Press, 1996.

McQuigg, Jackson. *Tampa Union Station*. Charleston, South Carolina: Arcadia Publishing, 1998.

Mormino, Gary R. and Anthony P. Pizzo. *The Treasure City: Tampa*. Tulsa, Oklahoma: Continental Press, 1983.

Mulder, Kenneth W. *Tampa Bay: Days of Long Ago*. Tampa, Florida: P & M Publishing Co., 1991.

Norman, Robert and Lisa Coleman. *Tampa*. Charleston, South Carolina: Arcadia Publishing, 2001.

Otto, Steve and Diane Schultz. *Treasures on Tampa Bay*. Memphis, Tennessee: Towery Publishing, 1996.

Pacheco, Ferdie. *Pacheco's Art of Ybor City*. Gainesville, Florida: University of Press of Florida, 1997.

Pizzo, Anthony P. *Tampa Town: 1824-1886*. Miami, Florida: Hurricane House Publishers, Inc., 1968.

Powell, Evanell. *Tampa that was. . History and Chronology through 1946*. Boynton Beach, Florida: Star Publishing, 1973.

Stoughton, Gertrude K. *Tarpon Springs, Florida: The Early Years*. Tarpon Springs, Florida: Tarpon Springs Area Historical Society, 1975.

Super Guide to Tampa Bay. Tampa, Florida: The Tampa Tribune, 1991.

Tampa: A Many Splendored City. Tampa, Florida: The Tampa Tribune, 1991.

Tampa: A Town On Its Way. Tampa, Florida: Junior League of Tampa, Inc., 1971.

This Was Yesterday: A History of Lakeland, Florida. Lakeland, Florida: Junior Welfare League, 1973.

Turner, Gregg. *Florida Railroads in the 1920s*. Charleston, South Carolina: Arcadia Publishing, 2005.

Vespari, Maria D. *City of Green Benches*. Ithaca, New York: Cornell University Press, 1985.

Waggoner, Holly. *Skyway To The Sun*. Sarasota, Florida: Omnigraphis Publishers, 1988.

Wynne, Nick. *Tin Can Tourists In Florida, 1900-1970*. Charleston, South Carolina: Arcadia Publishing, 1999.

Ybor City: City of Legend. Tampa, Florida: Tampa Preservation, Inc., 1996.

Young, June Hurley. *Florida's Pinellas Pensinsula*. St. Petersburg, Florida: Southern Heritage Press, 1996.

Index